KNOWING YOU
KNOWING ME

For a complete list of Management Books 2000 titles,
visit our web-site on http://www.mb2000.com

AUTHOR

Derrick White was born near Belfast, brought up in Dublin and lived in London throughout twelve years' Navy service. His career has included ambulance driver, navvy, salesman, health club boss, sales trainer, management consultant and Rotary Club speaker. His work in management training triggered a keen interest in psychometrics and personality profiling. His first three books were business books on sales, marketing and psychometric testing. He has lived in all corners of the UK, but settled in Scotland in 1972.

Twice, he stood as the Scottish Nationalists' Westminster candidate for Edinburgh East and in the Scottish Parliamentary election, he stood as the Scottish Socialists' candidate for East Lothian.

Between career moves, he worked for several seasons as a coach driver/guide for major tour operators such as Gray Line and Silver Coach Lines.

KNOWING YOU KNOWING ME

Why understanding personality is an essential Life Skill

Derrick White

2000

By the same author

Management Books 2000 Ltd

Close More Sales	1993
Success with Psychometric Testing	1998
Close More Sales (New edition)	2000

Neil Wilson Publishing Ltd

Scotland - Frequently Asked Questions	2003

First published in 2002 by Management Books 2000 Ltd
Forge House, Limes Road
Kemble, Cirencester
Gloucestershire, GL7 6AD, UK
Tel: 0044 (0) 1285 771441/2
Fax: 0044 (0) 1285 771055
E-mail: m.b.2000@virgin.net
Web: mb2000.com

Printed and bound in Great Britain by Biddles, Guildford

British Library Cataloguing in Publication Data is available
ISBN 1-85252-414-6

Contents

For Bernice

INTRODUCTION

Describing someone's physical appearance is easy. We have an abundance of useful adjectives; fat, thin, tall, short, dark hair, fair hair, no hair, blue-eyed, green-eyed, good teeth, no teeth, big nose, roman nose - the list is as long and varied as the people we describe. The advantage of physical descriptions is that they are quantifiable and we have constants as reference points. He was 6ft 2, weighed 190 lbs., ginger hair, blue-eyed, freckles and his nose and left ear looked like he may have been a boxer.

Very precise. A hundred people given such a description would pick out the same man in a crowd. Yet people's personality preferences and how they behave are more important than how they look. But when it comes to quantifying or measuring personality type, we have to rely on imprecise and often vague stereotypes.

- He was a typical accountant.
- He was a typical salesman.
- She was a typical actress.
- She was a typical social worker.
- He was a typical Sergeant Major.

To describe someone as a typical accountant may convey the intended meaning between people of similar views and who know each other well. But the risk is that the view is essentially a subjective view and may not be shared by the recipient. Assuming that the describer wishes to convey the image of someone as rather analytical, calculating, dry, unemotional and withdrawn; that image will only be conveyed if the description is shared by the listener. Accountants themselves will often tell you how they hate the term typical accountant with its pejorative implications. Quite right too. Sure, the intended imagery may describe some accountants but to bracket them all together is both imprecise and unfair.

Certainly, the accountancy profession does attract a certain personality type but it is much safer and wiser to establish the personality type first, put a clear handle on it and then use that as a descriptive term rather than use the profession into which they are drawn as the benchmark.

But I do not have a handle on the personality type, so I have to use the only exemplar I can think of to describe the image I wish to convey!

Fair enough, that is the purpose of this book, to give you the language of personality typing along with an understanding of what makes the various types tick, how they behave in given situations and how they interact with the other personality types.

Before we go on, let's just look at the pitfalls with one or two of the other paradigms above.

He was a typical salesman!

The common image which this is often meant to convey is of someone who is pushy, loud, talkative, back-slapping and hearty. My experience as senior sales trainer for the world's leading office equipment manufacturer finds the imagery quite contrary to the facts. All the top salespeople were calm, thorough, structured and very hard-working. They were all great planners and record keepers. They knew all their call ratios; calls to interviews; interviews to closing opportunities and closing opportunities to sales. The so-called 'typical salesman' tended to fly by the seat of his pants and was eternally optimistic but the high rejection rate which is the nature of selling could get him down sufficiently for him to give up. Whereas the successful salesperson saw rejection merely as a statistic or part of his structure of ratios and a stepping stone to his next sale. Or lastly …

She was a typical actress!

What do you mean? Oh, she was gushy, phoney, loved simply everyone, dahling - always saying we must have lunch but never got around to it, you know the type I mean. A complete assumption based on prejudice and a hostile view of a profession which has within it every personality type possible. We may remember more vividly the actress who gushed, or the salesman who couldn't shut up or the accountant who bored us to distraction at a party, but to use the profession as an exemplar of behavioural preference is unsafe and presents too many pitfalls for good communication.

To be fair, unless we have quantifiable, measurable, empirically proven terms or handles to describe certain personality traits, it is perfectly normal and reasonable to reach for the closest descriptive term we can think of. However the above illustrations underline how subjective and imprecise such random exemplars can be.

One example of how terminology can be used or misused is in the field of psychology itself. We use words such as moron, imbecile and idiot as interchangeable, but they do belong within precise brackets of measured intelligence, i.e. IQs of 50-70, 25-50 and under-25 respectively. Also descriptions of neuroses and psychoses tend to get jumbled up. Schizophrenia and manic depression are psychoses while phobia and hysteria are neuroses. Even schizophrenia is misunderstood - it is a splitting (Greek 'skhizo') of cognitive function from reality, not split personality which is a form of multiple personality, a neurosis. To be practical, in everyday layman's use, it is seldom necessary to fine tune our language but there are times when precision is all important. As a non-vital illustration, try going to your local garage and ask for some blue touch-up paint for your scratched car.

How will more precise terminology help?

In many ways. If you describe a man as 6ft 3, then everyone who hears the description shares exactly the same perception of height.

If you describe a man as tall, this will have many different implications depending on geography or nationality, as well as the height of the person given the information. Billy Connolly, Scotland's best known comedian, is known throughout Scotland as The Big Yin, or Big One. In the post war years in Glasgow before the National Health Service was established and before good nutritional practices were adopted, vast numbers of the poorer people were very small in stature indeed with the average height for a male worker at 5ft 6.

Anyone 5ft 10 or above was automatically called Big Yin. The 6ft Connolly when in Texas, Australia, Norway or any of the countries where good diet is the norm would have difficulty explaining why he was called big.

Where specifically can such terms be helpful?

Two fields - the professional and the personal.

In the corporate world, employers need yardsticks to measure many psychometric factors for a range of purposes including career guidance, staff selection, staff appraisals, assessment centres for promotion, team building and generally maximising human resources for optimum results.

In the world of personal relationships, it is immensely important to understand why we gel so completely with some people and why others alienate us. Understanding personality types helps us to communicate better with our partners, our children, our parents, our extended family, our friends and our neighbours.

Let's dwell on the professional. Recruitment has changed greatly over the years. Once references from previous employers were a major element of the selection process. In a more class-divisive and authoritarian age, references were often quite intimate and detailed. Employers did not shy away from all sorts of critical and pejorative comment. Now the law has changed greatly in favour of protecting the individual's rights and employers are reluctant to provide much more than the dates of employment, position held and salary details and perhaps one or two other hard facts. Personal opinion is now a rarity and often is only given where the ex-employer invites the prospective new employer to make contact by telephone.

Personality Profiling - or Psychometric Testing - is now standard practice in corporations world-wide. Because people change jobs more frequently and because references may be non-committal for fear of defamation, employers are finding that the onus for selecting and assessing personnel is entirely theirs. Consequently, the more accurate the systems available for achieving such appraisals, the more valuable they are to the employer. Bad recruitment decisions often take time to become apparent and are invariably highly expensive to rectify.

Another profound change in personnel selection processes is the nature of work itself. Manufacturing was once hugely labour intensive, with men (and it was mainly men) swarming through factory gates, so well captured in a Lowry painting. Now automation can drill holes, fit bolts to the correct torque and spray-paint an item in the time it would take ten men to open their toolboxes. Agriculture was similarly about manpower. Today a number of mammoth machines are moved onto the land at harvest time and acres of land are reaped in a day. Typing pools would consist of fifty or so young women neatly arranged in rows of desks with IN and OUT trays and virtually no freedom of expression whatever, with the added indignity of having to attract the supervisor's attention to be allowed visit the bathroom. Now a computer can produce more words per minute than an entire typing pool - with not a sheet of carbon paper or a typewriter eraser in sight. Entire accountancy and/or bookkeeping departments have been replaced by a software programme. No one cared if the girls in the typing pool were introvert or extrovert or one of Jung's Thinkers or Feelers. In the days of the old authoritarian style management (McGregor's X-style management - covered later) there was a worker-to-manager ratio of maybe fifty to one. It did not matter what psychological disposition an employee had. 'You are here to type, dig, assemble, shovel, paint, whatever - now get on with it. And when you've finished that task, let me know and I'll give you something else to do. If you cannot handle that, I'll soon find someone else who can.'

Since those dark days, there has been a sea-change in occupational focus. Vastly more people are now involved in service industries. Where we shop, which cafés, bars and restaurants we use and the products we buy, are decisions largely based upon the people who greet us and serve us. Thirty years ago, airlines switched the emphasis from routes and prices to the warmth and attractiveness of their hostesses. Remember, *'Hi, I'm Ellen - Fly Me!'* - with its unsubtle innuendo. But the message was clear, people and their personalities matter.

The number of aircraft manufacturers is limited. ISO (International Organisation for Standardisation) and ICAO (International Civil Aviation Organisation) rules ensure that all aeroplanes conform to strict guidelines or, more simply, one plane is very much the same as another, apart from Concorde but that only has appeal for Maslow's top of the Pyramid of Needs (see Maslow, A. qv.). Hotels are the same - mostly a 5 x 5 metre box with a shower, a TV, a phone, two sheets of writing paper (maybe three at a pinch) and a trouser press. Apart from the old ivy league of hotels, standardisation rules. In office equipment, photocopiers, faxes, computers and such like all look the same, have the same functions, the same dimensions and the same colour.

More and more, the discriminating factor in the world of goods and services is the people associated with them and their personalities. The other factor which has affected the nature of work is the rapidity of change. Huge multinational companies can pull out of a region with little notice. Corporations such as IBM, Mitsubishi, Motorola, NEC or Xerox have all been affected by the Sunrise and Sunset Industry syndrome. For several years, the world could not get enough TVs, computers, video-recorders or mobile phones and the manufacturing companies burgeoned like a sunrise. Then came the inevitable - in a word, sufficiency. Staff can be made redundant in their hundreds. Change is now endemic in industry. At the beginning of the last century, 96% of the world's shipping was built on the river Clyde at Glasgow. 'Clyde Built' became a term of recommendation on a par with 'as safe as Fort Knox'. The number of active shipyards there peaked at sixty-five. Now the remaining two or three yards are desperately seeking new orders to remain solvent. Meanwhile Korea, Taiwan, Hong Kong and latterly Norway are in the ascendant.

The frequency of changing jobs has shifted from the image of old Sam receiving his presentation clock after twenty-five years dedicated service to seven year intervals, to six, to five down to under four years in the industrialised west and still falling. So the need to advertise for new staff, recruit and train is more acute than ever.

As the turnover in staffing has speeded up, so has the recruitment process. Years ago, every letter of application was answered, most of the applicants were interviewed - often by two or more people. Today, all too often, negative replies are not made at all and if they are, they exude the dead language of pre-programmed computer-speak ... the calibre of applicant was high ... after careful consideration ... we regret ... you have not been successful. Those last words should be stricken from personnel people's vocabularies. The corollary of not being successful is you are a failure. You cannot be a failure if you have not even been interviewed. If people who work really hard pursuing a job are repeatedly told they are not successful, the accumulated negativity can undermine their confidence. Why not put it this way - there were over 200 applicants for the position and we decided to interview 10, so the only factor working against you was pure statistics. You could even add - we may have made a bad decision in not selecting you for interview. At least the applicant won't be put-down and lose heart.

Today's recruiter has to work faster. Most employers expect a high number of applications so they predetermine:

i) the skills, qualifications and experience required
ii) the personality profile best suited to the position offered.

The CV will indicate to a large degree how best (i) is matched and an interview with Psychometric Testing will establish the rest.

Elsewhere I have expressed disapproval at psychometric tests being used before an interview takes place. Unfortunately, personnel departments dealing with high volume applications may adopt this method. Another procedure which high volume recruiters prefer is demanding the completion of an application form. This may make life easier for the recruiter who becomes entirely familiar with the various pages and questions on the form. It does not make life easier for the applicant. Many people like to express their individuality through the medium of a letter and their own CV. They can highlight what they consider to be achievements and areas of their lives which they are proud of. They can express humour, strength, passion, distaste, preferences and a whole range of individual qualities. Even the way they construct sentences, their syntax and semantics can reveal a great deal about a human being. Forcing them to complete predetermined little boxes, like a credit card application, can be destructive to the recruitment process. The application form is an even greater irritant for the older person:

> *Years in Primary education?*
> *Dates?*
> *Subjects studied?*
> *Certificates awarded?*
> *Dates?*
> *Name of School?*
> *Address of School?*
> *Years in Secondary education?*
> *... and so on, ad nauseam.*

You know the sort of thing - pages of it. For a man or a woman in their 40s or 50s, it does not matter a damn what they did in a classroom 30 or 40 years ago. Further, everything educational has changed so dramatically, what possible relevance do such questions have! Many kids talk in a jargon which would have been unrecognisable forty years ago. They cannot spell or parse, they seldom read books, they cannot do long division, add up, recite multiplication tables or tackle any aspect of simple arithmetic without a calculator. But the larger corporations need conformity and bureaucracy. 'This guy's certainly not getting an interview - he didn't complete his Form AP934.' Maybe, the guy was brain-dead with exhaustion filling in all those superfluous boxes. He does not get an interview but he just happens to be the most decent, loyal, honest, honourable, conscientious human being you could meet in a month of Sundays.

Government officials and impersonal Personnel Officers in large organisations should read the above twice.

Any interview involves some form of selection criteria. One of the most basic thoughts floating through any interviewer's mind is, could I work with this guy? Perhaps not very scientific and some HR professionals might treat such a simplistic approach with disdain. But it is as good a starting point as any.

More sophisticated methods of psychometric evaluation have evolved including phrenology (head bump mapping) and graphology (hand writing analysis) which is still commonly used in France. Another was The Ink Blot Test where you were shown a sheet of paper someone had shaken a pen at. You were asked to describe any pattern or images which appeared to you. If you saw Coco the Clown with a big circular nose and bright eyes or the spots on some lovely affectionate Dalmatian pups you might be put in one category while if you imagined the Black Pit of Despair or the stains of sin on your immortal soul then you might well be placed in another bracket.

Not very scientific but the mouth is the floodgate of the brain and this test is very much a first cousin of The Word Association Test where you are asked to respond to a series of words fired at you by the tester. Clearly, if all your responses are very upbeat, positive, optimistic and cheerful, one personality profile can be gauged whereas if your responses are gloomy, despondent, macabre, negative and pessimistic, a more diametrically opposite opinion can be formed. That is at its most simplistic. More penetrative analyses can also be deduced from recurrences of similar words or themes.

In 1904, psychologist Alfred Binet and physician Theodore Simon developed the concept of 'mental age.' Professor HJ Eysenck went on to develop the definitive work on IQ. His book *Know Your Own IQ* was first published in 1962 when he was aged 36 and has been reprinted many times. The war years saw a rapid advance in the development of psychometric tests.

The brakes were applied in 1970 when a law suit was brought against an electric power company in the US for requiring an IQ test for a semi-skilled position. The US Supreme Court ruled that the test had nothing to do with the job in question, that it had been used to rule out certain ethnic groups from employment and therefore was illegal. The Court concluded that it had nothing against testing *per se* but the test must be job-related and content-valid. Having fired such a warning shot across the bows of US personnel departments, some disposed of all their tests, regardless of content validity for fear of lawsuits. But the need for tests wouldn't go away, so more tests were developed with a high focus on being job related.

On a training course I ran some years ago for salespeople with United Artists, one salesperson became quite defensive, uncooperative and hostile when I mentioned that at the end of the course there would be a test paper to check the absorption of course content. I could see there was something bothering this man, so I asked him to come for a walk during a lunch break. It transpired the man was dyslexic and he feared a 'fail' result and no job. In his role plays and practical work, the man was an excellent communicator, knew his product and its associated benefits and I felt he had what it took to succeed. I arranged to have a one-on-one test with me, where I converted the written test to an oral one. He sailed through it and went on to be one of the company's best performers. His paperwork in selling was not a problem as it was mainly the completion of little boxes and the buyers filled in their own personal details.

This is just one example of where a test was made directly job-specific, i.e. oral rather than written in the case of a sales person. A more narrow-minded manager might ask, What if the salesman has to submit a written proposal? Okay, fair point but the primary skill is getting as far as the request for a proposal and most sales organisations will happily find someone else to draft the appropriate submission for a potential customer. Also, these days, proposals tend to follow a company standard with only the relevant numbers needing to be inserted.

Personnel professionals have compiled many lists of criteria which they deem to be the most significant in the selection of personnel. Below is a list of the most recurrent, placed in a hierarchy of importance.

Intelligence and integrity
Structured interviews
Job knowledge tests
Personality tests
Assessment centres
Biodata

Conscientiousness
References
Years in education
Interests
Years job experience
Graphology
Age

Interestingly, age as a criterion came bottom of almost all lists (except in the rare instance where it was job specific). Thankfully, ageism is now illegal in the US and several European countries. The US has a number of strongly enforced anti-discrimination laws which limit the way organisations can use testing programmes for HR decisions. The most noted of these is the 1964 and 1991 Civil Rights Acts, the Americans with Disabilities Act (ADA) and the Age Discrimination in Employment Act (ADEA). In addition, many individual states have established 'Right to Privacy Laws'. In the hierarchy of factors listed above, other criteria such as; Years Job Experience, Years Education, Interests, References had no predictive power or more simply, it told us what the person had done but gave no indication as to what he or she would do in the future.

Frances R Berger, co-creator of the Berger Aptitude for Programming Test (B-APT) advises, *'it is quite possible to give job-related aptitude tests to people unfamiliar with the job'* ... but they should *'... simulate actual job tasks and require actual job skills'*.

One example might be the job of News-taker on a busy newspaper. These people were telephoned by reporters who may rattle off a breaking story. The News-taker had to record the facts accurately. In an interview, the first test for an applicant News-taker was to don a headset, listen to an audio tape and type the information as it was spoken. Accuracy had to be 94% or better and speed had to be commensurate with a normal speaking voice. All the CVs, interviews, panels, personality tests, biodata and conscientiousness in the world would be of no use if the basic News-taker test could not be passed. Once the employer is satisfied the applicant has the basics for the job, then personality may be probed along with reliability, health and all the other factors which determine all-round good performance

The field of psychometric testing is wide indeed. Though the word has become synonymous with personality testing, 'psychometric' literally means mind measuring so it can encompass tests for numeracy, literacy, IQ and competency in any number of skills. Strictly speaking, Personality Testing is just one form of Psychometric Testing.

Personality tests have been developed by Saville and Holdsworth, Myers-Briggs, Belbin, Thomas International, Wilson Learning and Margerison McCann, to name some of the biggest players. The focus of this book is on Personality.

Even the rather facile tests in the glossy magazines can be effective psychometric tests. *Just How Honest Are You?* taunts the magazine headline in bold scarlet letters or *How Faithful Are You To Your Partner?*

Then the questions:

You see a £20 note on the floor of your office building . No one else has seen it. Do you:

a) discreetly pick it up?
b) pick it up and intend to inform colleagues?
c) shout out immediately that you've found £20 on the floor?
d) stand on it and look around pondering on what you ought to do?
e) wonder if it is a trap ?

You know the type of thing. The only problem with such tests which directly challenge one's morality and integrity is, will the person be genuinely truthful?

The key issue is that all these tests are simply tools. Some are the perfect tool for a specific assessment, some are not. Some are the correct tool but placed in the hands of people who are ill-equipped to use them. Some employers buy in a personality test package and then require a consultant to advise on how it best be used. Why did they buy it in the first place? Because it is state of the art and all the popular management magazines feature such tests and frequently extol the importance of them. Sure they are valuable but so is brain surgery - or for that matter a TV repair kit - but optimum benefit can only be realised through the hand of the operator. Having heard so many bad experiences concerning psychometric tests, this is a good opportunity to list some dos and don'ts where psychometric testing means personality profiling

DO	DON'T
Consult with the appraisee and explain what the questionnaire entails.	Spring the questionnaire on the unsuspecting appraisee.
Stress that the appraisal is only one element of the interview process.	Usher the person into a little room and leave until the questionnaire is completed.
Stress that there are no wrong answers, like being left-handed or right-handed, it is purely to establish behavioural preferences.	Use vague reassurances like 'don't worry about it' or 'just be yourself'
Conduct an interview before any questionnaires are used.	Use words like 'test' implying pass or fail or that it has to be 'marked' evoking memories of the schoolroom.
	Allow the appraisee to think that questionnaires or tests are more important than human exchange.

Note: Forgive my licence but Appraisee is a word of my own coinage. It has the benefit of describing exactly what I wish to convey.

Knowledge is power and the person undergoing the Personality Test may feel vulnerable, intimidated, resentful, confused or hostile. The appraisee may feel a sense of violation, having answered up to 300 questions of a relatively personal nature. A worse scenario is where the 'test' precedes the interview. Some of the personality profiling systems in common use can take as long as an hour to complete yet the interview may only last 30 or 40 minutes giving the impression to the appraisee that the more important element of the interview was ticking boxes rather than human interaction.

Further, the appraisee may still be feeling resentful or subordinate during the interview and may possibly be distracted, mentally running over some of the questions, thus creating a demeanour not truly reflective of the individual's natural self.

Good management contains large elements of common sense and good manners. Alas, these precious qualities are not always in evidence in the work-place so, whether you are the appraiser or the appraisee, this introduction should help remove the mystery, the hostility and all too frequent mistakes and misunderstandings which accompany the world of Personality Testing.

1

Psychometrics - Another New-fangled Idea ?

When new terms enter our contemporary communication, it is not uncommon for us to go on the defensive and respond, *oh yeah, another new-fangled idea!* Human nature feels safer with what we know. How many of us swore we would never need, let alone buy, a computer, link up with the internet or the world wide web and acquire Information Technology skills. The video recorder, the DVD player, the cell phone, satellite TV, digital TV all met the same level of resistance from our conservative natures.

Similarly, with the non-tangible management training concepts, Maslow's Hierarchy of Needs, McGregor's X and Y styles of management, Adair's principles on team dynamics, Neuro Linguistic Programming (NLP) and Psychometric Testing - we recoil from smart-arsed academics who seem to produce complicated jargon relating to common sense situations.

The term 'psychometric testing' is both misleading and unhelpful. For a start, testing is associated with passing or failing. In various corporate situations, one can still hear the question 'how did you get on with your psychometric test?' The implication is clear, did you do well? You cannot do well in a psychometric test in the context of personality, you can only define your behavioural preferences. Granted, in a situation where an employer wished to recruit cool, analytical types and that was your natural preference, then it could be argued that you did well in a psychometric test. However in the field of human behavioural preferences, the word 'test' is unsuitable. Then take the word 'psychometric'. It sounds a mouthful and its meaning is not instantly clear, whereas 'personality profiling' sounds precisely what it is, a description or profile of personality.

As the word psychometric is the one most commonly used, we might as well translate it. The first half is from the Greek psyche for soul or mind and meter means to measure. So a psychometric test measures your mind/soul or, in this instance, your personality. To be pedantic, an IQ test, a literacy test, a numeracy test or almost any test of the mind may be called psychometric but the generally accepted contemporary meaning is measuring personality preferences.

New-fangled? Far from it. The term may put us on the defensive but the concept is as old as time. Man is a social animal. How we relate to our friends, family, bosses and colleagues is more important than the work we do. Scotland's finest comedian, Billy Connolly once described how he could not wait to get to work in the shipyards in Glasgow because of the wisecracks, banter and general hilarity that his sharp-tongued work-mates shared. Glasgow shipyards are pretty grim at the best of times - cold, wet, oily, smelly and often dangerous with the work itself being hard and unpleasant - yet Billy enjoyed the camaraderie and fun. Some of us are more people-oriented than others but all of us need human interaction to make life worth living. Good team spirit can make unpleasant jobs quite happy ones but bad human relations with incompatible or nasty people can make even the most attractive job seem unbearable.

In relationships, meetings, negotiations and committees, more dissent is experienced through a clash of personalities than through disagreement on substantive issues.

Therefore a knowledge of personality types and why they blend or clash is very much a life skill.

The assessing of personality traits is as old as society. We have always deemed the subject highly important, it is only that now we can identify clear, consistent, permanent and codified personality types and traits. This enables us to predict with a high degree of accuracy how a human being will behave in given circumstances. From this we can deduce how happy or unhappy the person will be in a given role, how productive or unproductive, how at ease or stressed the person will become. Nowadays we can make many deductions all based on empirically proven case studies. Though the analytical systems are now available, the wish and need to categorise people by personality type has always existed.

From earliest of times people with no knowledge of the science of psychometrics have used a huge selection of terms to describe personality.

Be yourself
He was a phoney
He's a real dark horse
She's always the life and soul of the party
Talk! She can't stop
The strong, silent type
Masterful
Dominant
Quiet and brooding
Earth mother
Tree hugger
He and I are poles apart
From a different planet
He doesn't suffer fools gladly - and so on.

Anyone of us could make a list of fifty personality descriptions without pausing for breath. They say the Innuits have more than thirty different words for snow. Why? Because it figures very prominently in their lives. Sailors don't want to be told it is windy - is it a half-gale? A gale? Force 8 or 9? Is it a storm? Force 10 or 11? Or is it a hurricane? The numbers on the Beaufort Scale make a huge difference when you are putting to sea.

So with descriptions of personality, that is why we have so many terms, because of their major importance to us.

We'll have a look at the earliest attempts to codify personality types in a moment but first, try this; fold your arms. Now unfold them and fold them in the opposite direction.

Difficult isn't it. Confusing. Awkward. Unnatural. At seminars when I have asked people to do this, there are some who are still windmilling their arms seconds after everyone else. One or two even give up.

Now try this - write with your normal writing hand the sentence '*the quick brown fox jumps over the lazy dog*'. Place the pen in the other hand and write the same sentence. Compare the two writing styles. One is normal, reassuringly familiar and you feel at ease with it. The other looks strange, jagged, forced, uneven, ugly perhaps. Similar effects can be achieved by swinging a golf club in the opposite direction to normal or changing hands with a tennis racquet. Unless you are one of nature's few gifted with ambidexterity, switching physical preferences will feel most unnatural.

If such physical preferences exist and are so strongly pronounced, it is not unreasonable to accept that psychological preferences exist. It was not uncommon for teachers in the first half of the 20th century to force left-handed children to write with the right hand. Conformity, stupidity and ignorant superstition all conspired to make children behave unnaturally. The very word 'sinister' acquired a wholly pejorative meaning yet it is simply Latin for left. Equally at fault, from a personality perspective, is the father who insists on making his son more extrovert and (as the father sees it) more tough and masculine, when the boy is naturally more reflective and more withdrawn. Physical and psychological preferences are acquired through the genes. Trying to change what comes naturally only causes stress and may cause a wide range of problems from loss of confidence, to stuttering, to an unbalancing of the mind.

Somos Como Somos

Somos Como Somos or *We Are As We Are* is the motto of one of Spain's leading Radio Stations. It is an ideal summary for the whole concept of playing to one's strengths. We cannot change but we can learn to maximise our natural gifts. A popular slogan used by painters, decorators and carpenters is *Don't Move - Improve*. So it is with natural gifts - we don't try to change what we are, we should learn to understand how we tick, then build on what we have.

Who was the first to give us labels?

'The Greeks Had a Word For It' was the title of a play by a little known playwright, Zoe Adkins. The phrase passed into everyday use because it encapsulates a truism, particularly for those involved in science or medicine. Most of the medical terms in use today have Greek roots and the father of modern medicine is accepted as Hippocrates (c 469 - 399 BC). Born on Cos in the Cyclades, he was the inspiration for Corpus Hippocraticum, a collection of the earliest Greek medical works. The name of the oath traditionally sworn by doctors takes its name from the same fifth century BC physician. It comes as no surprise that it was he who first put labels on the distinct personality types.

'Just give me the facts ma'am' was a standard line from the cop series Dragnet, spoken by the laconic Joe Friday. In any investigative work, it is essential to peel away the emotions and concentrate on the facts. When I ran a large department with a great deal of customer interface in United Artists, people would always bring me stories which began, with a hint of panic, *'There's a woman on the phone, really mad, just about sobbing, says she ...'* People always focus on the emotions first. I invariably said, just give me the facts, I can work out the emotions for myself. This woman is deeply upset, going ballistic, her TV blew up killing her pet cat. Just tell me about the TV and the cat - I can make the deduction for myself that she is not too happy.

So it was with Hippocrates and his fellow physicians. They found that although the symptoms of the various ailments they dealt with did not change a great deal, the manner of the patient could vary considerably. A tough, stoical and self-disciplined character might make minimal fuss about, say, an abdominal pain, whereas a more angst-ridden worrier might make the ailment sound like the Four Horsemen of the Apocalypse had visited him all at once. Though both had identical symptoms.

Hippocrates concluded that people were influenced by different bodily fluids. It may not be brilliantly scientific to 21st century eyes, but it is a great deal more rational than the astrological nonsense where different signs of the zodiac are said to be influenced by the displacement of the stars or the phases of the moon. Hippocrates' theory ran that those influenced by the four body fluids, bile, blood, phlegm and black bile all had distinctly different personalities.

His terms were:

CHOLERIC	**SANGUINE**
PHLEGMATIC	**MELANCHOLIC**

Clearly they made an impression as these terms are still in use today. Someone described as **Choleric** is said to be abrupt, irritable or, to quote Chambers Dictionary, angry or irascible. Shakespeare used the term biliousness in such a context.

Sanguine still means ardent, optimistic, confident and happy. **Phlegmatic** means calm, not easily excited. Only **Melancholic** has changed its meaning somewhat. Hippocrates originally used the term to describe pensiveness, reflection and a generally analytical or calculating disposition. Now the word is more associated with depression as in acute melancholia. However, dictionaries still give the meaning 'pensiveness'. So all in all, Hippocrates' four prime types have not changed since his time of identification. He called them:

THE FOUR HUMOURS

Although we associate the word humour with fun and laughter, the word is derived from the Greek 'to be moist' from which we take the English word humid. What Hippocrates was actually saying was the four moistures. We still use the word in the phrase, what kind of humour is he in? And someone can be in a bad humour as readily as a good humour. Hippocrates four types visiting his surgery with the same complaint would behave thus:

The choleric

'Hi Doc. Got this pain in the gut. I thought it would go away but I've had it a couple of days now. The wife thought it a good idea to see you. Can you give me a powder or pill and I'll be on my way.'

Brief even abrupt, direct, straight to the point, assertive. Here's what is wrong, fix it and I'll be out of here.

The sanguine

Morning, Doc. How are you doing? That girl, Helen, at reception is great, very welcoming, lovely manner, works like a Trojan. Geddit Doc? Helen, Trojan! Problem? Me? Well, not really a problem Doc, I've got this pain in the stomach. I'm sure it's nothing. Probably has something to do with the party I was at. If I'd one bottle of retsina, I had six. Helped wash down the double helpings of moussaka. What a night!'

Cheery, fun-loving, talkative, optimistic, buoyant and positive.

The phlegmatic

'Hello, Doctor, how are you? How is your wife Ariadne and little Hermes; what age is he now? My my, how quickly they grow up. Helen, lovely girl, tells me you are just back from your holiday on Lesbos, never been myself, though my Aunt Sappho loved it there - was it good? How can you help? Oh I hate to trouble you, but I have this pain in my tummy, similar to the one my sister Hermione had - she was never off the toilet poor dear - you gave her some purgative which seemed to do the trick. Mind you her husband Oedipus had it even worse but, between you and me Doctor, he was always a bit precious, a real mummy's boy ...'

The diametric opposite of the Choleric - Caring, considerate, sympathetic, concerned about relationships, self-deprecating.

The melancholic

'Good morning, Doctor. I'm a minute late, parking was difficult. Now I have this pain in the left lower abdomen. It started at 10 p.m. the night before last and throughout the night the pain developed from mild to acute. I took some analgesic tablets and an anti-flatulence potion which helped, but the pain is constant. My bowel movements are 33 per cent less frequent than normal. Passing of urine is normal. Blood pressure is 130 over 90 and my pulse which is normally 72 fluctuates from 75 to 81. No other symptoms to report.'

The diametric opposite of the Sanguine - formal, factual, detailed, accurate, analytical, low on intimacy, cool, precise.

Later on, we'll take a more thorough look at personality types and the terminology used today also an appraisal of how the different types interact with one another. One modern term worth mentioning now is the term *blind spot*. We already use in everyday speech such terms as, we were poles apart; we were chalk and cheese or diametric opposites. We may use these terms to allude to ranges of interests but most frequently we are highlighting personality preference differences or the means of expression rather than the actual subject matter. Opposites or blind spots do exist, so it is helpful to look at the four types in diagram form. You'll see in Figure 1 that Melancholic and Sanguine are blind spots for each other as are Phlegmatic and Choleric, literally diametric opposites.

4 **MELANCHOLIC** **Water**	**1** **CHOLERIC** **Fire**
3 **PHLEGMATIC** **Earth**	**2** **SANGUINE** **Air**

Figure 1 - The four humours

Hippocrates' four humours remained the bench-mark for defining personality for two and a half millennia right up to the 20th Century - apart from a correlation chosen by his contemporary Empedocles (c. 484 - 424 BC). Empedocles related the four personality types to the four elements, Fire, Air, Earth and Water. As the correlation is so complete, it is as well to take a look at the linkage.

The **Choleric** is certainly fiery, assertive, dominant, abrasive.
The **Sanguine** is distinctly airy, buoyant, optimistic, ebullient, light.
The **Phlegmatic** is clearly the earth mother/father, save the whale, caring, sympathetic.
The **Melancholic** has water qualities, cool, deep, reflective.

A further correlation of the period linked the four environmental factors, Hot, Cold, Dry, Moist which respectively reflect Choleric, Melancholic, Sanguine and Phlegmatic.

All these terms and relationships need not be remembered as we are about to fast-forward to the present and the more scientific Jungian terminology. However it is both humbling and fascinating to see that the ancient Greeks had as clear a working knowledge of personality differences as we have today. This is true of so many fields. We tend to believe that modern man's knowledge surpasses all others, yet only a glance at the architecture of the Romans, Greeks, Aztecs or any number of long dead civilisations should remind us how advanced they were. Egyptologists are still pondering on the wonders of the Pyramids.

How useful were the four humours to Hippocrates?

We cannot know for sure but it is a pretty safe bet that he and his colleagues would have annotated the medical records of their patients with an abbreviated code to denote which humour the individual identified with. Through understanding the personality of the patient, it would have been easier to get to the facts and reach the centre ground which might have been displaced or clouded by varying types and strengths of emotions.

It would also help them work with each other. Knowing that someone is by nature cool, distant and apparently aloof can assuage feelings of hurt or hostility. We are all familiar with the phrase, *Oh, it is just his way*. Often that is not good enough for us and we react with, *I don't care, it seems like damn bad manners to me*. The risk is greatest with the diametric opposites or blind spots. Sam Sanguine breezes into work in the morning - 'Hi everybody; morning Harry; hi Pete; how are you today, Liz - you're looking great ...' All respond with varying degrees of warmth except Melanie Melancholic who gives him a polite but restrained smile. Sam, like all Sanguines, needs to be liked and consequently thinks Melanie is a sour-faced and vinegary old maid. Melanie in turn considers Sam the classic empty vessel making the most noise, shallow, brash and loud. Neither is correct, of course, they just happen to be opposite poles, but our perception is our reality and how someone appears to us is - as far as we are concerned - how they are.

Perhaps more pronounced is the difference between the Cholerics and the Phlegmatics. The Phlegmatics are very caring, sympathetic and concerned about relationships. The Choleric can live without pleasantries, endearments, long preambles or subtle hints. Phyllis Phlegmatic will greet Colin Choleric with, *'Hello Colin, how was your holiday, did you go anywhere nice, did the family enjoy it ...'* Colin will respond with, *'Yeah it was fine'*, and he'll just walk on by. Colin is not being rude to Phyllis (though she, being a Phlegmatic, will be hurt by his brusqueness), he just does not see the point of small talk or all the social niceties to which Phyllis attaches so much importance. The Colins are very much gimme-the-facts people. Their story-telling will be a succession of dates, times, events and consequences - *'I was doing forty along East Street, came to the junction with North Street, put the foot down but a guy in a black BMW going south on North Street had the same idea ...'* The Phlegmatics need emotional embellishment - *'There I was on East Street in the rush hour and you know what the traffic is like, sheer hell*

- anyway, I'm late, I promised George I'd be home by seven sharp, you know what a cross-patch he can be when I'm late ...' You know the types. At seminars or lectures when I describe some classic elements of personality typing, there's always someone who says, You described my uncle/husband/wife/mother (you name it) to a T.

There are cultural differences and gender differences in personality profiling. For example, it could be difficult to tell apart an English Sanguine and an American Melancholic; also females are genetically more predisposed to the Phlegmatic than the Choleric but we will look at these factors later. Interestingly, it was Hippocrates who first recorded the theory that man is conditioned by his environment. He wrote (in perhaps not the punchiest piece of prose you ever read):

> 'The countries which have the greatest and the most frequent seasonal variations of climate also have the wildest and most highly diversified landscape and present the greatest array of mountains, forests, plains and meadowlands, while in countries where the seasonal variations are slight, the uniformity of landscape is at its maximum. Consideration will show that the same equations hold for human nature. Human physiognomies may be classified into the well-wooded and well-watered mountain type, the thin-soiled waterless type, the meadowy marshy type. Here too, there is the same effect on environmental variations on physique, and, if the variation is great, the differentiation of bodily type is increased proportionately'

Takes a moment to digest but you get his drift. We can extrapolate from the above that if physiognomies can be environmentally conditioned so can psychological disposition. It is not surprising that street exchanges in Scotland can be abrupt and terse while in Madrid or Milan people shake each others hands, kiss, embrace and enquire after not only the individual but the entire family. If you are standing on an Edinburgh street corner with a freezing North Easter blowing the rain horizontally into your blue-tinged face, the inclination to dally awhile and exchange pleasantries, even with the nicest people you know, is somewhat suppressed. The sense of urgency to get from place to place is more pronounced in northern climes, whereas the philosophy of mañana is so much more appropriate where the heat of the day brings activity to a halt.

A refreshingly humane element of Hippocrates' character is that he never alludes to racial stereotypes, an appalling corrosive habit which has pervaded society especially through the 20th Century. Some of the old English Punch Magazines of a hundred years ago depicted other races as lazy, dishonest or stupid. The Irish came in for the most vitriolic attacks, consistently portrayed in cartoons with simian features. The British establishment was hostile to Irish Home Rule and the oldest propaganda trick in the book when you don't like an ideal, is to vilify the idealists. Civil rights activists, Jews, Blacks have all been victims of bitter supremacists. The cultural traits of Afro-Caribbeans, Asians, Latins and others have all borne the brunt of white western feelings of superiority. The only flaw in Hippocrates 'conditioning' theory is that similar environments do not necessarily produce similar cultures. But here a whole new dimension could be explored such as religious influences - and that opens an entirely different can of worms.

Enter Carl Gustav Jung

Not much is recorded on any significant advances in the field of psychology or psychometrics from 400 BC until the beginning of the 20th century. There is some evidence that the earliest written psychometric tests were used for civil service positions in ancient China. As Confucius, the great Chinese philosopher, died ten just ten years before Hippocrates was born and Chinese culture was most enlightened, it is not unreasonable to accept the probability. It is said that the test took the form of asking the applicants to write poetry. So civilised and logical. How someone expresses his or her thoughts and feelings in lyrical form would certainly give us an insight into their literacy, grasp of scansion, expressiveness, emotional depth and the more aesthetic side of their nature. But for hard, documented records of psychometrics we have to leap forward to the 20th century.

Jung was born in the July of 1875 in Switzerland. As a young man, he was keenly interested in the spiritual and spiritualism. He could hardly fail to as his father was a clergyman as were no fewer than eight of his uncles along with his maternal grandfather. This latter pastor was also said to be regularly in contact with the spirit world. Weekly he conversed with his deceased first wife while his second wife (Jung's grandmother) and his daughter (Jung's mother) listened in. The things people got up to before TV!

Jung's earliest playgrounds were churches and graveyards and the vehicle he was most familiar with was the hearse. Comics and Biggles were not for this kid, no sir. For light entertainment, he devoured medical text books and books on philosophy especially those by Friedrich Nietzsche (1844-1900) and Immanuel Kant (1724-1804). He reflected deeply upon life and death, body and soul, good and evil, light and dark, order and chaos and other human dichotomies. Also, the dual religious influences of Swiss Protestantism and pagan spirituality made Jung aware of a dualism within himself. He believed he had two different personalities which he named 'Number One' and 'Number Two'. This in turn led him to the conscious and the unconscious and ultimately to psychiatry.

Interestingly, the first psychometric tests (as we know them) were produced in 1904 - when Jung was only 29 - by Alfred Binet, a psychologist and Theodore Simon, a physician. They constructed a test for children consisting of problem situations. The answers could be scored objectively and they were the first to develop the concept of mental age. For example, when an examinee's test score was equal to the arithmetic mean (or bench-mark) of the scores of five-year-olds, that examinee was said to have had the **mental age** of five, regardless of the **actual age**. Later on, psychologists defined the IQ as the ratio of mental age to **chronological age** computed as **IQ = MA/CA x 100.**

Psychometric testing took on a greater significance during WWI and WWII where the recruitment and training of a vast number of men required greater speed and efficiency. Here Jung played a part by pioneering the principle of **word association** tests where the analyst fires a series of words at the subject asking him to respond with the first word which comes to mind. Many a comedy scene has been built around this concept but even the layman can detect a personality pattern evolving with each successive word response.

Jung's four functions

Those psychometric tests which deal with personality profiling, as opposed to numeracy or literacy, use a language which is wholly Jungian in origin. Jung as we know was deeply interested in the dual nature of man's psyche. He propounded that there were two primary divisions and four primary functions in the human psyche.

He coined the words **extrovert** and **introvert** to describe **attitude**. His definition of extrovert was where energy flows outwards towards the world and is motivated and oriented by external objective factors, while introverted energy withdraws from the world and is motivated and oriented by inner, subjective factors. Our generally accepted understanding of the words is more simple. Illustrations are always helpful. Most of us would see Bill Clinton as an extrovert and Richard Nixon as an introvert. Jung would probably agree with us though his explanation might be more complex than ours.

Jung observed that we **perceived** the world in one of two ways; either by **thinking** or **feeling**. Having perceived the world, we then make **judgements** about the world through **sensing** or through **intuition**.

Jung consistently chooses to highlight the dichotomies in the human psyche. As we saw, it was his interest in the spiritual - life and death, good and evil, yin and yang, which led him to psychiatry which focuses on the **conscious** and the **unconscious**. Where the latter two become out of kilter, one is said to be mentally deranged, which is a psychiatric term for psychosis. In his evaluation of personality, we have dichotomies again. The very word psyche is itself a dichotomy as it means both soul and mind. Not only in the psyche do these dichotomies exist but physiologically our brains are made up of left brain and right brain, each half controlling differing functions and the motor movements in opposite sides of the body.

Jung's Dichotomies

- We are all somewhere on a line drawn between extrovert and introvert.
- We all perceive the world through either thinking or feeling.
- We all make judgements about the world through sensing or intuition.

Thinkers are said to perceive the world through observation, reflection and contemplation; whereas **feelers**, as the name suggests want to explore, investigate and examine. This is most noticeable in children; the thinking child can sit quite happily in a corner with a book or a toy and remain relatively quiet. The parent, particularly one who already has a feeling child, every so often checks to see if the child is all right. 'Are you okay?' the parent asks with a degree of concern. The thinking child looks up with a calm and perhaps serious face and replies, 'Ah ha' or some other utterance of contentment.

Now the feeling child is quite different. This kid is into everything, under the kitchen sink, into cupboards, into the sewing box, the desk, you name it. Lids get unscrewed, tubes get squeezed, packets get opened, contents are spread on the floor, felt for texture, licked for taste. The child is not being bad, mischievous or naughty, the child is being a classic feeler.

We have all experienced both types of children. When parents have both types they often cry out in exasperation, 'why can't you be more like your sister/brother?' The answer is simple, they cannot. This is a clear division in personality preference. If you draw a line and calibrate it with markings 1 to 10 and place thinker at one end and feeler at the other end, your personality preference will lie somewhere on that line and place you in one hemisphere or the other.

Similarly with sensing and intuition. Let us define them first. **Sensors** are those whose personality preference is to make judgements through the senses, by touch, smell, visual observance, taste and sound. **Intuitives**, although capable of sensory perception, by nature choose to rely on gut feeling and instinct. A typical example of these two functions at work could be the interview. The Sensor checks any references, reads the CV thoroughly checking for chronological sequence, examines any academic or skill qualification certificates and needs to be satisfied that all the appropriate documentation is in order. The Sensor will also absorb all the personal details from the physical presence of the interviewee - manner, posture, vocabulary, dress, deportment and so on. Questions are more likely to be job specific. After the interview, the Sensor will ask the Intuitive, 'What did you think?' The Intuitive might reply, 'No, not what we are looking for!' This can infuriate the Sensor who will complain, not unreasonably, *'You didn't even read the CV or look at the references and as for the questions you asked, for heaven's sake, about football, fishing and - of all things - what sort of movies he liked'*. The Intuitive's defence will sound weak and insupportable to the Sensor. *'There was just something about the guy I didn't like'*.

We are all familiar with this dichotomy as well. Joe brings Bill home for a meal, a few beers and to watch the big game. Afterwards Joe asks his wife how she liked Bill. *'I've got to be honest, Joe, I didn't like him one little bit, nothing specific, there was just something about his manner, I couldn't take to'*. Joe of course protests, telling his wife what a great guy Bill is and dismisses her discomfort with, *'Ah, but just wait till you get to know him'*. A few weeks later Bill absconds with serious amounts of the company's money at the same time owing Joe a few hundred pounds which he had borrowed to tide him over. We all have similar stories.

Apart from the Sensor/Intuitive dichotomy, women are naturally much better readers of body language than men. Another example is the two couples out together for dinner. Afterwards one wife says, *'They must have had one hell of a row earlier'*. *'Oh?'* says her husband blankly. *'Don't tell me you didn't notice their behaviour to one another!'* *'No...'* says the husband rather defensively *'...they seemed okay to me.'* The wife had noticed (often subconsciously) all the little subtleties, nuances, gestures, mannerisms and phrasing which give off strong signals to the intuitive or reader of body language.

One explanation for this is that women are genetically predisposed to interpret body language because of their role in bearing children.

To a man, a baby's cry is a crying baby, whereas a woman can interpret a specific signal.

Investigative police work will utilise both Sensors and Intuitives. In the notorious case in England of the Yorkshire Ripper, Peter Sutcliffe had murdered thirteen women, all of whom he believed to be prostitutes. The amount of Sensor work that went into the investigation was prodigious. Vast areas were scrutinised, distances were measured, bus stations, gas stations, cafes and every possible source of information was checked, re-checked and checked again. In excess of a hundred thousand people were questioned. Sutcliffe himself was questioned on no fewer than nine occasions. Facts, facts and more facts were assessed, so much so that the senior police officer in charge of the case worked himself into a condition of serious ill-health. In the end it was an Intuitive cop who just had a hunch about Sutcliffe. He followed his hunch which in turn led him to follow the path of the murderer's vehicle where he found the very hammer which had been used to break the skulls of so many unfortunate women.

Personality preferences are gifts. Who is more valuable, the Sensor or the Intuitive? The Extrovert or the Introvert? The Thinker or the Feeler? Certainly in some circumstances one may be more useful than the other, but overall they are all equally important.

EXTROVERT ------------------------------- INTROVERT
THINKER ------------------------------- FEELER
SENSOR ------------------------------- INTUITIVE

Figure 2

Probably the quickest psychometric test possible would be to ask someone to mark a point along the three horizontal lines above indicating where that person believes he or she stands in relation to the six personality factors. However, although the pen-work would be brief indeed, the foregoing explanations would have to be understood before embarking on relating oneself to the six factors.

Of the four functions, one will be the superior or the most differentiated function. By changing the permutations of the two attitudes (extrovert and introvert) and the four functions (thinking, feeling, sensing, intuiting) Jung derived eight distinct personality types. There is no need to try to remember these or use them as benchmarks. We are going to look at simpler and clearer terminology in the chapters which follow. The following eight terms are featured purely in recognition of the seminal work carried out by Jung.

1. Extrovert Thinker
2. Introvert Thinker
3. Extrovert Feeler
4. Introvert Feeler
5. Extrovert Sensor
6. Introvert Sensor
7. Extrovert Intuitive
8. Introvert Intuitive

We'll be returning to the personality types throughout the book but perhaps a thumb-nail sketch of each would be helpful to be getting on with.

1. Extrovert Thinkers

Scientists, economists - people who have that reflective, analytical capacity but who go on to produce theorems, formulae and treatises. They are interested in order and material facts.

2. Introvert Thinkers

Philosophers - people who formulate questions and seek to understand their own being and the questions of our time. May neglect the world and dwell on their own ideas.

3. Extrovert Feelers

Show business people, chat show hosts - they are concerned with personal and social success, outgoing, buoyant, talkative.

4. Introvert Feelers

Monks, nuns, musicians - they come across as harmonious, self-sufficient, calm, often charismatic.

5. Extrovert Sensors

Builders, architects, speculators - practical, realists, sensual, may have weaknesses towards earthly pleasures.

6. Introvert Sensors

Connoisseurs, aesthetes - where the extrovert sensor needs tactile or sensual contact, these people can internalise their pleasures; they are often unassuming and bemused.

7. Extrovert Intuitives

Media people, public relations people, advertising people - expressive, creative, keen on novelty, restlessness may denote future instability.

8. Introvert Intuition

Mystics, poets - they follow an inner vision, day-dreamers, may be gifted in clairvoyance, may see themselves as misunderstood geniuses.

This is heavy stuff

You're right, but is important to stress that much of this chapter has been devoted to Jung, his language and terminology and his interpretation of the personality preference because it is only right to give the man his due. However, in the 21st Century, the Jungian personality types have been defined much more clearly particularly with reference to the world in which we live today. For example, using Type 8 - Introvert Intuition. Does anyone know any poets or mystics? Although the archetype (another of Jung's terms) is correct, for it to be of any constructive use to us we need to relate the type to the environment we work and live in now.

I think I could identify the types without Jung

You probably could. You know you can drop into conversation easily with some people while with others it is like drawing teeth. You know that when you have a problem, some people will put an arm round you, care for you, give you sympathy and an uninterrupted hearing, whereas others might tell you to pull yourself together or not to be so damned soft. Some never come out of their shell and with others you wish to heaven they could go back into it.

Whenever any philosophy or theorem is codified and laid down, we tend to be less impressed than we might, often because the inherent truth of the theory is something we have recognised and been aware of. We do not need Isaac Newton to tell us that when a rubber ball is dropped from a height of six feet it will not bounce as high as a ball dropped from twenty feet. However, we do need his calculations to work out the rate of acceleration of a falling object.

We all know that people are motivated by differing factors and at different levels. We have all met the guy who changes companies because he is offered a flashier car or a managerial title or some other ego-related goodie. We understand the elation the salesman feels when at the big, brash conference he is hailed as best producer of business in the land. The applause from his peer group and his superiors along with the award of a movie star holiday at some exotic location gives him more satisfaction than perhaps a pay rise. However it took Abraham H Maslow to define and codify mankind's **Hierarchy of Needs**. When we read it, we find the hierarchy so simple and so obvious we wonder how Maslow acquired such fame for his definitive theorem.

Maslow reckoned our first base was survival. We needed food and drink. Once fed and watered what did we need? Somewhere to be safe and secure. A dry cave perhaps. Okay we're fed and watered, got somewhere to shelter and sleep, what next? You guessed it. A mate, someone to love and share with. With hunger at bay, a nice pad and a mate to share it with our aspirations leave the physical and shift to the psychological; we seek status and, having experienced that, we want to be the head honcho, the big cheese, the VIP. And, of course, you cannot go up a layer until the one you are on has been satisfied. A pretty logical progression, one whose inherent truth we almost certainly knew - but, it took Maslow to lay it out in a tried and tested theorem.

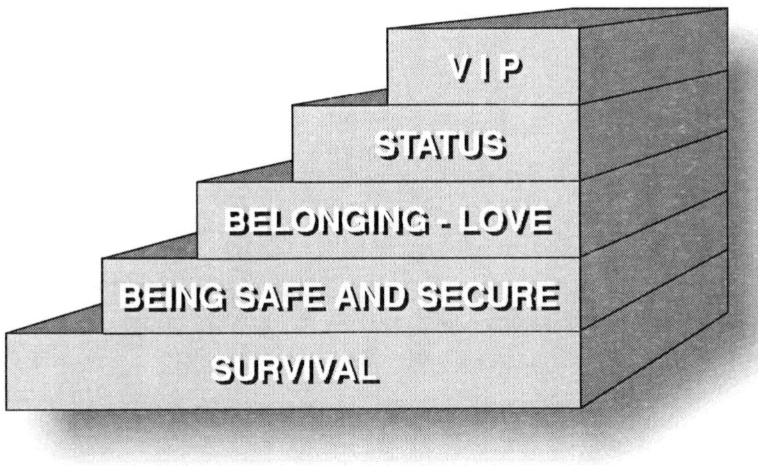

Figure 3 - Maslow's Hierarchy of Needs

Simplistic as it may seem, Maslow's hierarchy has been universally accepted and its principles applied in many ways. It can influence management strategy. Large institutions with extensive buying budgets will allocate furniture to staff in accordance with an internal pecking order. The height of the chair-back, the width of the arm-rests, the upholstery material, the desk surface area, one pedestal or two and so on - all will vary depending not so much on need but on seniority. Paradoxically, the CEO will often have the largest desk with two deep pedestals, yet he will have the least need. Not long ago having the key to the executive washroom was a sure sign one had arrived.

Perhaps the most common application of Maslow is in advertising. Just look at the car adverts. *Survive* - ABS braking systems, air-bags, road-holding, crumple zones. *Safe, secure* - suspension, upholstery, finish, anti-theft devices. *Belonging, love* - the head- turning effect of the design, the romantic settings, the cool stereo and CD. *Status* - the middle to high price tag, the limited numbers, the Italian styling, the top of the range model. *V.I.P* - the seriously up-market marques, Rolls Royce, Porsche, Ferrari. In a purely logical world, no-one would buy a car capable of three times the speed limit. One watchdog body, the

Advertising Standards Agency of Great Britain, recently instructed one car manufacturer (MG) to discontinue an advert which focused solely on speed. The entire ethos of the advertisement was, Can you handle the adrenaline rush? The sub plot? Do you want to show off? Do you want to turn heads? Are you man enough? Pretty unsubtle, even infantile stuff in a post-James Bond era. Maybe, but Maslow's Hierarchy is not a temporary fashion - its strength lies in defining human nature.

All car adverts employ each level of Maslow by rotation. How safe it is one week, how fast it goes the next, then how economical, how stylish, the macho qualities, the feline graceful qualities, how impressive in the drive or at the golf club. All focusing on human fallibility, vanity and weaknesses.

How does this connect with the four quadrants?

The direct relationship is that we might tend to see Jung's defining of personality (or Hippocrates' for that matter) as something we already felt we knew - just like with Maslow or Newton's laws on gravity. We also know that when the bath is too full and we immerse our 200lb body in it, the water is going to spill over the sides, but it took Archimedes (yet another Greek) to calculate the precise relationship between the amount of water displaced and the weight of the body immersed.

The beauty of empirically proven theories or laws is that we have a constant. We know that a certain personality type in a given situation will behave in a wholly predictable manner. The FBI have a Behavioural Sciences Unit and the 'mad bomber' of New York in the 1950s, James Brussel, was finally nailed through personality profiling. Sure we are all conscious of different personality types but only in a general cognitive sense - we had no guidebook. With applied logic, experience and intelligence, most people could find their way around London, but they would take a few wrong turnings, miss several sights worth seeing and perhaps waste time in areas not worth the journey. However with an accurate guidebook, we know where we are and can make precise directional decisions again and again.

There is another personality link with Maslow and that is a predictable correlation between the levels of the hierarchy and the personality types. For example, using Hippocrates' four humours, the VIP and Status levels might appeal more to the Cholerics and the Sanguines, whereas the Love and Belonging aspects might appeal more to the Phlegmatics. Advertisers are well aware that there are plenty of Melancholics out there who just love the long list of specifications (look at some of the computer ads) while their diametric opposites, the Sanguines, prefer the big picture - what will it do?

In the terminology of Sales Training, the specifications are **features** and what it will do for the buyer are the **benefits**.

Using one other quite different product as an exemplar, when Smirnoff Vodka was first launched in the US, the marketing people tried several angles from its exoticness to its purity but sales never took off. It was only when the winning idea of social acceptability was employed that sales began to rocket. The strap line used was *It Takes Your Breath Away* and the message was clear - a few drinks at lunchtime or on the way home will not result in boozy breath.

In the next chapter, you will be asked to assess your own personality profile, so we will say no more on the various archetypes lest it might prejudice how you look at the personality profile questionnaire. Once you have open-mindedly and accurately identified your own personality type we can then show how that type interacts with other types, why you feel comfortable with some and ill-at-ease with others. The great benefit is that when you reflect upon relationships where you felt compatibility or hostility you will understand why those reactions existed. It helps to make sense of ourselves, our families, our colleagues at work, why teams gel and why some disintegrate. In short it helps us understand people.

2

Getting To Know You

Having read the Introduction and Chapter One you will already have decided that you will lean towards one of Hippocrates' Four humours and no doubt you will have placed yourself somewhere along the lines between extrovert and introvert, thinker and feeler, and sensing and intuitive. As you now feel you know roughly where you are on the psyche map, why not pause for a few minutes and let us pinpoint your personality preferences with a high degree of accuracy.

It is a very straight forward questionnaire of 25 questions. Each question has four options. One is most like you and one is least like you. You may pause for a moment on one or two questions and think, 'none of the four options is really like me'. This is not uncommon but while none might be truly like you, one will be the most like. Rather like four foods or four movies, you might think, 'I don't like any of them'. Fine, but one is going to be closer to our preferences than the others. We have all been hungry, perhaps on a journey, and we finally find a diner with a limited menu of dishes we don't really care for. We will normally pick something.

Take for example Q11 - Are you (a) sociable and enjoy others' company, (b) tolerant and patient, (c) self reliant and strong or (d) accurate and correct. It could be that you consider yourself all four but one will be most like you and one least like you. Like Olympic sprinters, it may need a photo finish but one should be a nose in front.

The same principle applies with the least like questions. You might feel that all options are a bit like you, but one will be least like you. In the unlikely event that you genuinely cannot make a decision, skip the question entirely. A perfectly thorough and accurate personality profile can be derived from a questionnaire with one or two questions omitted.

The benefit of this questionnaire is that you are going to self-score the outcome and no-one other than yourself need share your profile with you. One risk with formal appraisal testing in the work-place is that we can be tempted to 'tick the box' which matches best how we would like others to see us. This is utterly pointless. It is rather like a sprinter claiming to be a long distance runner or vice versa. One race in the wrong event and the truth becomes glaringly obvious.

So pen poised, in your own time, off you go. Average completion time is 12 minutes so a few minutes over or under is fine. However if you seem to be taking an inordinately long time, it could be that you are being too self-conscious and self-analytical. Remember somos como somos - we are as we are.

Firstly mark MOST like you with 4 - then LEAST like you with 1.

1	Considerate of others	____
	Withdrawn and reflective	____
	Determined and forceful	____
	Outgoing and boisterous	____
2	Demanding, rapid	____
	Helpful, caring	____
	Charming, talkative	____
	Perfectionist	____
3	Dynamic, challenging	____
	Incisive, must be right	____
	Emotional, friendly	____
	Painstaking, quiet	____
4	Thoughtful, formal	____
	Encouraging, accepting	____
	Assertive, driving	____
	Life and soul of the party	____
5	Unassuming, kindly	____
	Flamboyant, excitable	____
	Decisive, abrupt	____
	Distant, slow to intimacy	____

6	Co-operative, agreeable	_____
	Stubborn, combative	_____
	Fun-loving, restless	_____
	Logical, unexcitable	_____
7	Sticks to principles	_____
	Analytical, unemotional	_____
	Overbearing, leader	_____
	Easily distracted	_____
8	Sincere, trustworthy	_____
	Brave, unafraid	_____
	Undemonstrative, resigned	_____
	Good mixer, enjoys company	_____
9	No self-doubt, forceful	_____
	Soft-spoken, formal	_____
	Articulate, gregarious	_____
	Accommodating, agreeable	_____
10	Suspicious, wary	_____
	Generous, willing to share	_____
	Persuasive, convincing	_____
	Bombastic, task driven	_____
11	Sociable - enjoys others' company	_____
	Tolerant and patient	_____
	Self-reliant and strong	_____
	Accurate and correct	_____
12	Spontaneous, impulsive	_____
	Trusting, loyal	_____
	Thorough and detailed	_____
	Strong-minded, pushy	_____
13	Pedantic, deliberate	_____
	Responsive, affectionate	_____
	Authoritative, bossy	_____
	Demonstrative, indiscreet	_____
14	Irrational, challenging	_____
	Passive, soothing	_____
	Results driven	_____
	Methodical, disciplined	_____

15	Controlling, competitive	_____
	Questioning, self-controlled	_____
	Disorganised, unstructured	_____
	Loyal, Supporting	_____
16	Unyielding, argumentative	_____
	Slow to anger, peacemaker	_____
	Cool, dutiful	_____
	Enjoy fun and games	_____
17	Warm, friendly	_____
	Win at all costs, do it my way	_____
	Detached, studious	_____
	Extrovert, noisy	_____
18	Exuberant, loud	_____
	Confrontational	_____
	Willing to help and listen	_____
	Cautious, quiet	_____
19	Good-natured, pleasing	_____
	Inspiring, optimistic	_____
	Tough-minded, gutsy	_____
	Calculating, observant	_____
20	Lenient, not over-strict	_____
	Reserved, slow to decide	_____
	Original, individualistic	_____
	Sociable and cheerful	_____
21	Compassionate	_____
	Introspective	_____
	Goal oriented	_____
	Team oriented	_____
22	Ebullient, enthusiastic	_____
	Single-minded	_____
	Restrained	_____
	Humane	_____
23	Dislike weakness	_____
	Sympathetic	_____
	Undisciplined	_____
	Calculating	_____

24	Contemplative	____
	Quickly decisive	____
	Feeling	____
	Need recognition	____
25	Detailed	____
	Relaxed with strangers	____
	Unafraid to confront	____
	Dislikes structure	____

Now you can score the results.

Refer to the questionnaire pattern below and you will see that every question has one of four options shown by a single letter - D, I, S or C.

1	Considerate of others	S
	Withdrawn and reflective	C
	Determined and forceful	D
	Outgoing and boisterous	I
2	Demanding, rapid	D
	Helpful, caring	S
	Charming, talkative	I
	Perfectionist	C
3	Dynamic, challenging	I
	Incisive, must be right	D
	Emotional, friendly	S
	Painstaking, quiet	C
4	Thoughtful, formal	C
	Encouraging, accepting	S
	Assertive, driving	D
	Life and soul of the party	I
5	Unassuming, kindly	S
	Flamboyant, excitable	I
	Decisive, abrupt	D
	Distant, slow to intimacy	C
6	Co-operative, agreeable	S
	Stubborn, combative	D
	Fun-loving, restless	I
	Logical, unexcitable	C
7	Sticks to principles	S
	Analytical, unemotional	C
	Overbearing, leader	D
	Easily distracted	I
8	Sincere, trustworthy	S
	Brave, Unafraid	D
	Undemonstrative, resigned	C
	Good mixer, enj company	I
I9	No self-doubt, forceful	D
	Soft-spoken, formal	S
	Articulate, gregarious	I
	Accommodating, agreeable	C
10	Suspicious, wary	C
	Generous, willing to share	S
	Persuasive, convincing	I
	Bombastic, task driven	D
11	Sociable - enj oth comp	I
	Tolerant and patient	S
	Self-reliant and strong	D
	Accurate and correct	C
12	Spontaneous, impulsive	I
	Trusting, loyal	S
	Thorough and detailed	C
	Strong-minded, pushy	D

13	Pedantic, deliberate	C
	Responsive, affectionate	S
	Authoritative, bossy	D
	Demonstrative, indiscreet	I
14	Irrational, challenging	I
	Passive, Soothing	S
	Results driven	D
	Methodical, disciplined	C
15	Controlling, competitive	D
	Questioning, self-controlled	C
	Disorganised, unstructured	I
	Loyal, supporting	S
16	Unyielding, argumentative	D
	Slow to anger, peacemaker	S
	Cool, dutiful	C
	Enjoy fun and games	I
17	Warm, friendly	S
	Win at all costs, do it my way	D
	Detached, studious	C
	Extrovert, noisy	I
18	Exuberant, loud	I
	Confrontational	D
	Willing to help and listen	S
	Cautious, quiet	C
19	Good-natured, pleasing	S
	Inspiring, optimistic	I
	Tough-minded, gutsy	D
	Calculating, observant	C
20	Lenient, not over-strict	S
	Reserved, slow to decide	C
	Original, individualistic	D
	Sociable and cheerful	I
21	Compassionate	S
	Introspective	C
	Goal oriented	D
	Team oriented	I
22	Ebullient, enthusiastic	I
	Single-minded	D
	Restrained	C
	Humane	S
23	Dislike weakness	D
	Sympathetic	S
	Undisciplined	I
	Calculating	C
24	Contemplative	C
	Quickly decisive	D
	Feeling	S
	Need recognition	I
25	Detailed	C
	Relaxed with strangers	S
	Unafraid to confront	D
	Dislikes structure	I

Say for Question One above, you chose the first option as most like you (Considerate of others) and the third option as least like you (Determined and forceful). The Translating Key shows this as S (Most Like) and D (Least Like). Note D, I, S or C against all your chosen answers.

Then count up the number of Ds, Is, Ss and Cs. Which are Most like you and Least like you. Maybe put them in a box, like so:

	D	I	S	C
Most like	2	7	11	5
Least like	16	5	2	4

If, for example, you considered yourself one of Hippocrates' Phlegmatics, you will find that in your Most column, you will have a lot of the letter S (Sympathetic Supporter). You will also probably have relatively few D's (Driver), the diametric opposite of S (see fig.5.). If you rate yourself a High-S you will have very few S's in your Least like box and probably quite a lot of D's in your Least like box.

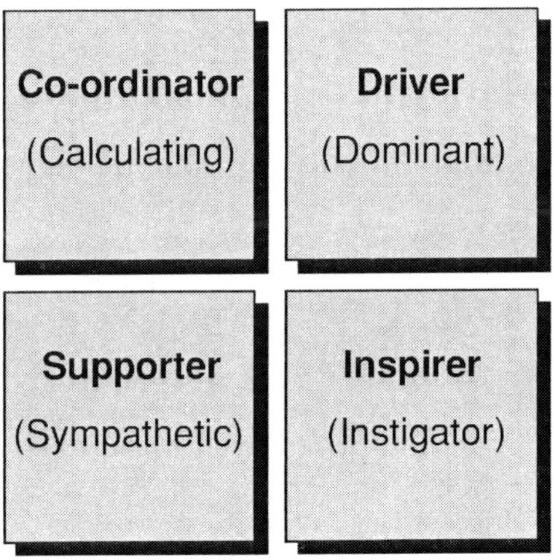

Figure 5

What's with this DISC? Why not ABCD?

Sorry to ask you to produce a result which is not immediately apparent. The reason is this - if DISC was explained thoroughly beforehand, it might - just might - create a bias to predispose you towards one letter or another. It is wiser to ask you to complete the questionnaire naturally and without prejudice and then explain what the resultant DISC profile means.

You ask why DISC and not ABCD? Fair question, it could be almost any four letters or indicators. Hippocrates codified the Four humours and Jung identified the Four Functions and generically in the field of personality psychometrics, the term is **Four Quadrant Behaviour (4QB).** At its simplest, all psychometricians accept that there are four primary factors which make up human personality preferences.

The most common four indicators in use today are DISC, which stand for **Driver, Inspirer, Supporter, Co-ordinator**. Like Hippocrates' Four humours, they are laid out above (figure 5) in the same four quadrant (4QB) style. (You may also see DISC standing for Dominance, Influence, Submission and Compliance)

There are now literally hundreds of systems being used to assess personality and there are many descriptive terms used to put a handle on each personality type. However, virtually every system in use accepts that there are four base types. Some systems subdivide the four further - into eight types or sixteen types but they all agree on four as the base. Rather like a painter's palette with four primary colours, the mixing of the four colours will give an almost infinite number of differing shades. Several systems actually choose to use colours e.g. Red = Dominant Driver, Yellow = Sunny Inspirer, Green = Caring Supporter and Blue = Cool Analytical Co-ordinator. Other systems use animals to denote the qualities, e.g. the Driver might be an assertive bull, the Inspirer a playful dolphin, the Supporter a good-natured labrador and the Co-ordinator a thoughtful owl.

Some say that one system of indicators is superior to another. The case for DISC is that it is the most common of the indicators used. One advantage of using colours is that colours are non-judgmental. If you describe someone as High-D or a Driver, that may have unattractive connotations to some and sound complimentary to others. Whereas if you say someone is a typical Red or a typical Green - it is very hard to find offence or compliment in either. Ironically, the very word 'typical' has acquired a certain pejorative resonance as in the angry wife's comment, that's just typical of you!

So DISC is recommended because these four categorisations are the most commonly used in everyday personality typing. Some people find the four elements of Fire Air Earth and Water the most easily memorable and, to their thought processes, the most descriptive. Others feel more comfortable with the four colours, especially when it comes to subdivisions, for example, they say it is easier to say someone is a Greeny Blue rather than a Supporting Coordinator or a Yellowy Red rather than an Inspiring Driver. You choose.

Just to help with the correlation of the different descriptive terms, this little table may help as an aide memoire:

Choleric	Sanguine	Phlegmatic	Melancholic
Fire	Air	Earth	Water
Driver	Inspirer	Supporter	Co-ordinator
Red	Yellow	Green	Blue
Bull	Dolphin	Labrador	Owl
Dominant	Expressive	Amiable	Analytical
Assertive	Buoyant	Caring	Detached
Intuitive thinker	Intuitive feeler	Sensing feeler	Sensing thinker
Thruster	Involved	Caring	Loner

The result of your self-scoring questionnaire should show that you have a majority of one of the four letters D, I, S or C. Let us say for example of the 25 choices to select the adjectives most like you, you might have chosen 11 Ss, 7 Is, 4 Cs and 3 Ds. This would place you very firmly in the Supporter quadrant.

Okay, so I assess myself very much as an Inspirer with Driver as close second, so what can I learn about myself?

What are the characteristics of the four personality types (4QB)?

Let us list the four archetypes in the sequence D, I, S and C.

Driver

Drivers, as the name implies, are people of action. They are decisive, quick, assertive and lack self-doubt. They are not afraid to challenge ideas and the modus operandi of others. Although they do not intend to be rude or brusque to others their assertive and abrupt manner may seem ill-mannered to others, especially those of the diametric opposite quadrant. Drivers dislike unnecessary discussion or waffle. At meetings, they grow impatient with formalised structure; they grasp the objective of the meeting and wish to see a quick, decisive conclusion. By being assertive, they seek control of situations and frequently are found in positions of control. They tend not to dwell on past bad decisions but wish to move forward to the next situation requiring action. The force of a Driver's argument may make others resentful but where the latter may feel offended for some time afterwards, the Driver will have forgotten the incident entirely.

Strengths:	Competitive, determined, purposeful and strong-willed. Though a touch macho in style they are usually fair-minded and do not quibble over trivial issues.
Weaknesses:	Can be impatient, abrasive, intolerant, argumentative and aggressive.
Common Roles:	Managers, military commanders , sales, positions of authority
Jungian terminology:	Extrovert Intuitive Thinkers

Inspirer

While the Driver is the one who gives the command, the Inspirer will convey the command to the troops, sell the idea, seek team spirit commitment and encourage and inspire the troops to get on with the job. Inspirers are impulsive, out-going, talkative, optimistic, positive, sociable, fun-loving, gregarious and demonstrative. They can motivate others by their dynamism and enthusiasm. Terms like *life and soul of the party* and *a real party animal* were coined with Inspirers in mind. Inspirers can be flighty with both people and ideas, leaving them to explore others when their interest wanes - which can happen quite quickly. Their flightiness may at times appear shallow to others - particularly those of the diametric opposite quadrant. Inspirers are very much 'big picture' people who can rapidly welcome a new idea without examining the minutiae.

Strengths:	Positiveness, persuasiveness, optimism, sociability, sense of fun.
Weaknesses:	May be flamboyant, hasty, impetuous, indiscreet, can be too keen to be liked, dislike for prolonged concentration on a single task. May appear flippant and insincere especially to blind-spot quadrant (Co-ordinators). Tendency to show-off. When you tell a joke, the High-I is more likely to be searching for another joke than concentrating on yours.
Jungian terminology:	Extrovert Intuitive Feelers
Common Roles:	Sales, team leader, reception, holiday courier, People oriented.

Supporter

Supporters are the blind-spot for Drivers. They are calm, easy-going, sociable, caring, sympathetic, patient and tolerant. They prefer harmony to assertion and co-operation to authoritarianism. They are concerned very much with people, feelings and relationships. They are noted for their pronounced ability to listen to others. They tend to see the ethical and moral value of an action or policy. Though outwardly passive, their disposition is to be principled and loyal but in a non-confrontational way will take a stand on a matter of conscience.

Strengths:	Loyalty, tolerance, understanding, patience,

	humanity and the ability to encourage and share with others.
Weaknesses:	May seem bland, passive, non-assertive even docile. May also appear negative and in some circumstances stubborn.
Common Roles:	Social work, nursing, personnel, medicine
Jungian terminology:	Introvert, Sensing Feelers

Co-ordinators

Are the blind spot of the Inspirer. Where the Inspirer will stand back and admire the mosaic work of art, the Co-ordinator will want to take a closer look at the individual pieces. Co-ordinators are cool, analytical, reflective and slow to make a decision. As one of Jung's Sensors, they like evidence, hard facts and details. On buying a car, the Co-ordinator would want details of specifications, engine capacity, brake horse-power, ABS system, safety features, paint tones and warranties. The Inspirer would be more likely to whistle and say, what a beaut! Co-ordinators are also in Jung's Thinking hemisphere therefore their preference is to observe and assess with a level of detachment. Very difficult to sell an idea or product to at first attempt. Their preference is to be accurate and the information that they seek and that they give will tend to be precise. In the art gallery, the Inspirers are that ones that stand back and say, Wow! while the Co-ordinators are the ones moving in for a close-up. It is worth stressing here that the 'big picture' view and the 'close-up' view are not exclusive to any one quadrant - they are only preferences.

Strengths:	Attention to detail. Ability to concentrate on a given task without interruption and usually get it right. Reluctant to give an opinion until all the facts have been assessed - (on occasion can be a weakness as well)
Weaknesses:	Too formal, distant and detached. May appear indecisive, suspicious May seem cold, reserved and undemonstrative.

Common Roles: Scientists, accountants, engineers, lawyers, technical specialists.

Jungian terminology: Introverted, Sensing, Thinkers.

So, if I am in the Inspirer quadrant with Driver as close second, do I assume that my main tendency is to be all the qualities shown for Inspirer but that I am quite capable of adopting the Driver's qualities when called upon?

In a word, Yes. This is where so many of the Personality Profiling companies opt for the subdivision into eight or even sixteen types. With DISC we can drop into eight subdivisions (or more) quite easily.

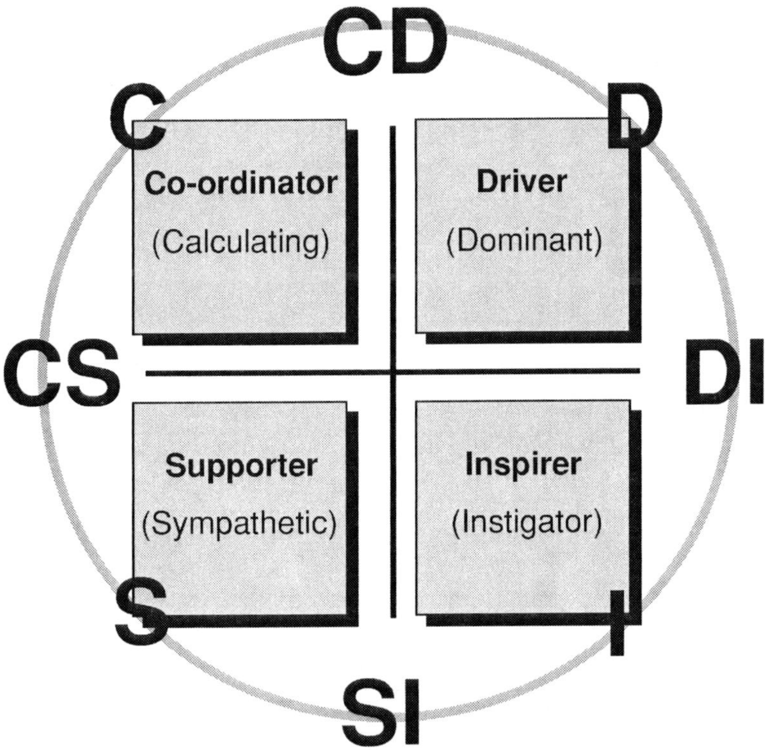

Figure 6

In figure 6 you can see the four base quadrants, D, I, S and C but where they meet on the border at - to use compass points - North, East, South and West we have the meeting points CD, DI, SI, SC. So someone who has a personality profile result of equal scores of Inspirer and Supporter could be called an SI (or IS for that matter). In the vast majority of personality profile results one quadrant is superior. So where possible it is best to work with the base four.

To continue the compass point analogy, all sailors know there are 360 degrees in a circle and North, East, South and West are expressed as 000, 090, 180 and 270. Although your compass course may be 280, for every day communications, the description would be sailing West. *(Wait a second, a Co-ordinator at the back with his hand up. Yes? You'd always say 'steering 280'. Okay thank you)*

In summary, the point is that you need never be stuck for a profile type. *He was a D; She was a High-S; He was a typical C* and so on. If you are stuck for a subdivision then use the compass points. *He was a real mix of C and D.*

Among psychometricians, one of the quickest ways of identifying a personality type is to present it in graph form. Below is an example from which you can see at a glance the profile is High-I, Low-D and S and very Low-C

Of the 25 opportunities to identify most with D the appraisee chose 4
Of the 25 opportunities to identify most with I the appraisee chose 16
Of the 25 opportunities to identify most with S the appraisee chose 4
Of the 25 opportunities to identify most with C the appraisee chose 1

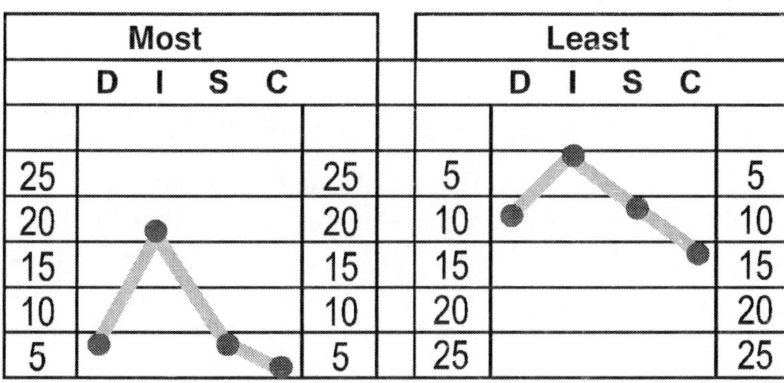

** Please note the Least graph is inverted to allow it to relate to the rises and falls of the Most graph.*

Of the 25 opportunities to identify least with D the appraisee chose 7
Of the 25 opportunities to identify least with I the appraisee chose 1
Of the 25 opportunities to identify least with S the appraisee chose 6
Of the 25 opportunities to identify least with C the appraisee chose 11

The above figures were chosen completely at random in an illustration as to how you may wish to lay out your own self-scoring profile. The graphs above are not precisely drawn nor intended to be state of the art exemplars. To produce your own all you need is a ruled note book or sheet of paper and just mark off 5 horizontal lines to allow scoring from 0 to 25. Often Human Resource files will have a simple pencil sketch, even without lines, just so long as the peaks and troughs are in a reasonably accurate relationship to one another- e.g.

Figure 7

You can tell at a glance this is someone who is High-D, with S as second preference and I and C neck and neck for 3rd and 4th.

But surely the MOST and LEAST are mirror images of each other?

Very fair comment and in many circumstances they are. In the two graphs above, the lines of both graphs are quite congruent. However this begs the question, why bother to have a Most and Least at all?

There is a distinction. The Least graph is an indicator of your **Natural Self** and the Most graph is an indicator of your **Persona** (yet another Jungian term). Persona is the Latin word for a player's mask and Jung used the word to describe how we adapt to or deal with the world. Psychometricians use the term generally to describe how we conduct ourselves in the workplace. For example, one of nature's

High-Is who went to work as a mortician would find that the Inspirer graph line was significantly lower on the Most graph.

How can this be? Surely, as you said earlier, 'Somos como somos', and, if we are honest, the peaks and troughs should match?

Perfectly reasonable assumption! However quite intensive research established that we will answer Most and Least questions slightly differently. At its simplest, we tend to be more natural and at ease with the Least questions because we are not stating a positive. We are not stating this is the definitive ME. We are rejecting and that process is easier and more natural. If you look over the questionnaire again, you'll see that you made quite quick choices on the Least Like selection. *H'mm, let's see, that's not like me, nope, that's not a bit like me - tick!*

But when we come to the Most Like decision, we are fractionally slower and an element of self-consciousness is brought to bear. No it is not intentional, there is nothing phoney about it, we tend to think of our place in the world and how we react to it and how it reacts to us. Sometimes the two graphs blend precisely, rather like the two above, for example a natural High-I / Low-C in a High-I / Low-C job will have congruence in those two quadrants. But someone with naturally Low-D who is placed in a management position with maybe a staff of a dozen people will find the D graph line is higher in the Most graph than in the Least (Natural self) graph.

We all have to adapt to some degree. A naturally High-C boss who is happiest number crunching and attending to the details of running a business will have to practise communication skills with staff and ask them questions about their family, their holidays, their hobbies and so on, otherwise the working atmosphere would be too sterile and cold. Conversely a High-I boss might enjoy mixing with staff, having fun, party nights and so on, but knuckling down to studying the accounts, the business turnover and the hundred and one pieces of detail which can determine the success or failure of a business is an absolute necessity, however much the preference is to be one of the team.

So your Least Like graph is your Natural Self and your Most Like graph is your adapted style or Persona.

One of the great health risks in the modern world is stress and one way of identifying its existence is through a personality profile. We will return to this and the uses to which personality profiling can be put, but first we'll have a look at some archetypes.

Great ! Graphs, questionnaires, systems, their evolution and the technical terminology are all very well but what about people?

Okay. Yes, one could deliver a day-long seminar on sex appeal but a few pictures of Marilyn Monroe, Racquel Welch or Kim Basinger could make the point a tad quicker - as could, of course, Mel Gibson, Harrison Ford or Hugh Grant. *What was that at the back? Oh I see -* ***none*** *of them do anything for you!*

Real life examples of Drivers, Inspirers, Supporters and Co-ordinators

Without the accuracy of proven psychometric tests, using real life examples has its risks. However, many prominent figures display the characteristics we associate with the four types in 4QB or the eight types outlined in figure 6.

• DRIVERS

As a well-known figure, one of the most clear cut Drivers in modern history was Margaret Thatcher, Prime Minister of the UK from 1979 to the 90s. They say that for a woman to succeed in a man's world, she has to be twice as good as the men around her. This PM was decisive, assertive, impatient, dominant, single-minded, authoritative and firm. She radiated all the qualities which make up the Driver profile. A very High-D. The two contiguous quadrants are C and I but if she leaned towards another quadrant, it was the C and not the I. She had very little sense of humour, did not like parties and found all the chatter, gossip and heartiness that went on at parties boring and unnecessary. Her leaning towards the C quadrant is evident from her background in chemistry. She appeared to have a very low S count and one finds it difficult to see her as the come-to-momma type. Her rather sour-faced son could reflect an absence of kisses and cuddles as a child (see nature v. nurture)

The previous UK Prime Minister to display these forceful qualities with such clarity was Churchill. Another prominent High-D from the UK is Northern Ireland's Ian Paisley - never known to be diffident or hesitant, always overwhelmingly assertive and domineering to the point of aggression.

John Wayne displayed all the qualities of the don't-mess-with-me Driver, so did James Cagney. Barbara Stanwyck, Bette Davis and Joan Crawford all had that assertive persona which gave their roles such charisma.

Eisenhower? Not entirely - although a D, he was more a DC (due North) with a combination of the assertive General, which he was, with the more analytical and reflective qualities of the Co-ordinator.

Jack Kennedy? Again, plenty of D but probably on the DI line (due East) as he had the gift of oratory which is very much an Inspirer's quality along with the capacity for being very personable and charming

• INSPIRERS

Both Bill Clinton and Ronald Reagan appeared very much in the Inspirer quadrant. Smiling, friendly, hand-shaking, back-slapping, quick to laugh, easy, optimistic and buoyant. There are cultural differences throughout the world and the US has always had a soft spot for Inspirers as leaders. The bluff, easy, hand-shaking, open, look-you-in-the-eye type has always had an appeal for citizens who regard those qualities rather much as American qualities. Being highly intellectual, aesthetic, cultured or sophisticated, though not a minus, have never been a great plus. No-one could argue that Ronald Reagan was an intellectual but people liked him and even gave him a second term. Similarly with Clinton, the Come Back Kid or the Teflon man. He had one or two skeletons in his cupboard (stains on his record was the term that came to mind but the use of stains seemed a little indelicate) but again people liked him. Inspirers are good conversationalists and orators and both Clinton and Reagan were first class public speakers. Psychometricians use a one-line quip; *generally speaking, Inspirers are generally speaking.*

An unlikely Inspirer is the Dalai Lama, a charming man with a wonderful sense of fun and mischief. Why unlikely? Just a form of prejudice really, as we in the West tend to associate religious leaders from the Orient as deep, reflective, ascetic mystics. Without evidence, it is a risk to assume, but the Dalai Lama's profile would probably be closer to an SI, as he displays in equal amounts the qualities of a caring Supporter. We don't need too many examples of the Inspirer as they are the easiest to spot. At any party, listen to where the most noise is coming from and somewhere in the centre will be the current Danny Kaye, Robin Williams or Eddie Murphy.

• SUPPORTERS

When Margaret Thatcher was finally ousted by the UK's Conservative Party, her chosen successor was John Major. Whether it was because Major was from the quadrant which is diametrically opposite Thatcher's is hard to say, but it is a safe assumption that it was a contributory factor. The bossy, domineering, impatient Driver, Thatcher, had outlived her use and it was time for change. Major was ideal as an opposite, a Supporter - amiable, friendly, pleasant, courteous, modest and affable. Later in his premiership, Major's outspoken denouncement of those who plotted against him - he called them bastards - might have seemed untypical but Supporters care about relationships and will take a stand on matters of principle. The cricket loving PM had a strong sense of fair play. Again, during the

2001 UK Conservative Party's leadership contest, Margaret Thatcher endorsed the Co-ordinating Driver (Ian Duncan Smith) candidate while John Major gave his support to the High-I candidate (Ken Clark). Major took the opportunity to take a few swipes at Thatcher in the process focusing on her disloyalty to him after he had succeeded her. Not very Supporter-like? Actually it is. Supporters are slow to anger but they have a strong sense of loyalty and will take a stand on a point of principle. It was John Major's very sense of decency which clearly made him so hostile to those who would undermine him.

Western movie women were often portrayed as High-S. The gal in the gingham dress happily sweeping out the log cabin, making bread, working the water-pump and uncomplainingly doing all the chores, never seemed to mind when her man (usually a monosyllabic High-D) rode home after weeks away on the trail or in the saloon. A High-D Bette Davis wouldn't have stood for it. Dramatists love opposites - another example was the ultra High-S Olivia de Havilland who played the sister of the High-D Scarlet O'Hara in Gone With the Wind. Dramatists also like the clash of two High-Ds, one of the reasons Gable and Leigh sparkled so well in the same movie.

Pursuing the Presidential link, Jimmy Carter displayed strong Supporter-like qualities - courteous, amiable, friendly, compassionate and ethical. When in office, Carter's rather bleeding-heart admission (to some) that he had committed adultery in his heart had the hallmark of a High-S. His later denunciation of George W Bush, may have come as a surprise to some, not associating condemnation with Mr Nice Guy. But Carter saw Bush's reneging on the Kyoto Agreement then withdrawing from the Ballistic Missile agreement as dishonourable acts and Supporters will take a stand on a matter of principle. Carter's reaction to 'Dubya' Bush is very much on a par with Major's hostility to Thatcher. Both genuine nice guy Supporters but both quite prepared to stand up and be counted on matters of conscience.

• COORDINATORS

The French seem to have a preference for High-Cs as their leaders. Giscard D'Estaing, Pompidou and Mitterand all displayed C qualities - cool, detached, formal and reserved. Compare with the demonstrative Clinton. Against their normal pattern, the US chose one memorable High-C, Richard Nixon. High-Cs have excellent qualities - thoughtful, reflective, precise, accurate, attentive to detail and so on, but their downside includes traits such as suspiciousness, caution, introspection, defensiveness and uncommunicativeness. As the heat was turned up on Nixon over Watergate, he began to show all the unattractive qualities of the High-C. Perhaps we should get this into perspective; Watergate was not a hanging offence, sure it was seriously indiscreet, and very bad form but how many politicians would refuse as a point of principle to eavesdrop on the opposition in an election year? Some of the nasty character assassination which goes on in politics and some of the disreputable funding are more reprehensible than bugging the neighbours. But with so many situations in life, it is not the problem but how it is handled.

Nixon as one of Jung's Introvert Thinkers didn't look at the big picture as Bill I-did-not-have-sex-with-that-woman Clinton would have done. Nixon focused on the mosaic piece, he psychologically closed ranks, became suspicious and began to distrust everyone around him, finally internalising his emotions so greatly that he made that rambling and totally introspective speech about not having Nixon to kick around any more. Who can forget that sweaty, disjointed, self-obsessed delivery on TV. The High-I Reagan probably would have owned up, told the American people that some of his boys were out of order, shrugged his amiable shoulders, focused his innocent grin at the cameras and the people would have responded, Ah, what the hell, it's no big deal. History has afforded a level of sympathy to Nixon which is not misplaced. Nixon's mishandling of Watergate totally eclipsed his pioneering dialogues with Communist China. Jack Kennedy almost became an icon - certainly in the land of his ancestors, many Irish homes had a picture of Kennedy alongside the Pope or even in a threesome with The Sacred Heart. Which man was the more moral, Kennedy or Nixon? No doubt history will pass judgement, which is one thing a personality profile cannot do. The jails are full of all four quadrants - the only imbalance might be in the type of crime committed, e.g. the High-Ds might figure more prominently in crimes of violence.

As a political footnote on Co-ordinators, a contemporary of Richard Nixon's in the UK was Prime Minister Harold Wilson. Wilson also displayed some High-C qualities. He developed what amounted to an obsession with the media, particularly the BBC. He constantly challenged the BBC's evenhandedness and had staff monitor the numbers and nature of references to himself and his party. Denis Healy (Wilson's senior minister) writes in his autobiography, *The Time of My Life,* that when Wilson retired in 1976, 'he was no longer plagued by the demons of jealousy and suspicion which had tormented him in his first two Governments'. Tormented by jealously and suspicion - transpose the words into a biography of Nixon and the blend would be seamless.

3

The Power of Personality Profiling

There is none so zealous as the convert and I openly admit that my earliest introductions to what was always referred to as Psychometric Testing made me very sceptical of the whole business. Now, with long contemplative hindsight, I can see exactly why. Not only did I not fully understand what the methodology or purpose was of such tests but one of three other elements was also seriously wrong.

- The people introducing the Test packages did not properly understand their own product ... or
- they did understand it but lacked the communication skills to convey all the features, advantages and benefits to me ... or
- I was too dim or slow on the uptake to grasp all the applications and benefits.

After countless lectures and articles, and a couple of books on the subject, it now matters little which of the three went wrong. Maybe it was my fault but I have resented not grasping the principles outlined in this book and *Success with Psychometric Testing* sooner. They are so enormously helpful in dealing with people, enthusing people, mollifying people, confronting people and just generally handling people. Stressed in the Introduction is the fact that, since the beginning of time, we have been describing personality traits, simply because they are so important to us. Just recently in one of the more substantial Situations Vacant supplements in the national press, there was an advert from a major blue chip company and it read:

We're not interested in your qualifications, we're interested in your qualities!

An unusual angle, but you understand their drift. *So you've got a certificate testifying you can add and subtract (or whatever) but what contribution can you make to drive our company forward?*

Personality has always been a key issue with us - we really feel we know someone from their behaviour or, as St Matthew's gospel has it, 'by their fruits you shall know them'. To use the New Testament link - St Peter comes across as a High-I, always wanting to be close to Jesus, seeking friendship and approval. When the disciples are out on a boat on the Sea of Galilee, Jesus appears in the early hours of the morning walking from the shore across the water towards the boat. They see him and are frightened but Peter calls out, *'Lord, if it is really you, command me to walk on the water to meet you.'* Very High-I, spontaneous, extrovert, demonstrative. Jesus says go for it. Peter can't wait (High-I, impulsive, impetuous, adventurous) he immediately strides out (optimistic, needs recognition). Out on the water he starts to lose confidence and begins to sink (High-Is can bite off more than they can chew). Jesus bears him up.

Would St Thomas have launched himself across the waters? Not a chance. The New Testament tells us that after Jesus was crucified, he arose after three days and appeared to his disciples. All fell to their knees and worshiped. Thomas (who had been absent) was adamant that he needed evidence - one of Jung's Sensors, probably a Sensing Thinker, a High-C - his stand was firm. Not until he had examined the nail wounds on Christ's hands and placed his own hand into the wound left by the spear on Christ's side would he believe in The Resurrection.

Some teachings tend to be critical of St Thomas for lacking faith. The pejorative term 'Doubting Thomas' has passed into the language implying that someone fails to grasp a self-evident fact. Quite unfair. Thomas, as a High-C would quite naturally be hesitant to accept such an overwhelming suspension of the natural law. How many of us whether D, I, S or C would accept without question the sheer majesty of the Resurrection. Jesus in his, as Christians would have it, infinite wisdom, wholly understood Thomas and invited him to fulfil his evidential requirements, giving us one of the more powerful lines in the entire Bible where Thomas fell to his knees and with utter humility whispered, *My Lord and My God.*

Using people as exemplars is much more interesting than making references to types, particularly Jungian types - *'he was a typical Extrovert Intuitive Feeler'*. Oh was he? Wait a minute till I work that out. *'He was a real Robin Williams.'* Okay, got ya!

During one lecture someone asked, 'in which quadrant would you place Jesus?' The short answer is nobody can be sure of any historic character, we can only make intelligent deductions from what evidence we have. For a Christian who believes that the Bible is the word of God and therefore that Christ was divine, the answer to the 4QB question should, logically, not be too difficult. If you accept that Jesus was wholly man and wholly God, then it is not unreasonable to place him in a wholly human context, i.e. that he embodied all quadrants. It is unlikely that an omnipotent, omniscient God would pigeon-hole himself into a D, I, S or C bracket. The New Testament would seem to bear this out. The *Gentle Jesus Meek and Mild* - to quote that dreadful 18th Century hymn lyric by Charles Wesley - was the same Jesus who was so enraged by the money lenders in the temple that he physically threw them out, roaring at them, 'my house is the house of prayer, you have turned it into a den of thieves'. The same Jesus who had such enormous compassion for Lazarus, Mary Magdalene, the blind, the lame and the diseased; yet again the same person who often chose to be solitary and deeply reflective. Here we have pronounced amounts of D, S and C. The remaining quadrant, Inspirer, could in a religious context be used as a term of reverence for Jesus. How many people could exhort us to abandon all our worldly goods and follow them.

Attitude - the determining factor

How many stores, showrooms or restaurants have you walked out of because you were disappointed by the staff's knowledge? None - it is always their manner.

Let's put the question into perspective. In my sales training courses, I gave salespeople as many exercises and role plays to do as possible. Sales managers tend to recruit a high proportion of High-Is - this is not incidentally a recommendation it is just the way it is. It stems from the old concept that good salespeople have the gift of the gab, always ready to rattle off a spiel, great hand-shakers, back-slappers and so on. Remember the adage that, *generally speaking, High-Is are generally speaking,* and you'll see the need to keep these people involved. Talk at them for too long and they get restless. One exercise I included wherever possible was this:

I would ask them all to assume they had been appointed as the sales manager. It was now their job to advertise for, interview and recruit a sales force. Now - write down five or six things you would be looking for in the applicants. As the salespeople busied themselves with their notebooks I quietly went to the flip chart and drew a large T on a blank sheet. Like figure 8 below.

When they were all finished I would go around the room asking for a word from each list. Invariably the large T ended up looking like this:

Enthusiasm	
Persistence	
Smart appearance	
Determined	
Hard working	
Punctual	
Good team player	
Helpful	
Conscientious	
Confident	
Philosophic	
Cheerful	

Figure 8

Sooner or later someone would ask, 'what's the T for?' I would explain that it was to write something on the other side. 'Like what?' Something which doesn't fall under the bracket which all these words on the left fall under. 'Oh, and what's that?' As a clue I would put a large **Q** over the left hand list and a large **S** over the right hand blank column. Seldom, if ever, did anyone grasp the division. I had to explain it.

On the left, the Q stands for qualities and the S on the right stands for skills. Not one of you have chosen any skills, every one of you has chosen qualities. The moral of my story was simple. You don't have to have certificates, high intelligence, great numeracy, great literacy or - as you illustrate - any skills at all. Simply develop the right **attitude** or **qualities** and you can be as successful as you wish.

Ray Kroc, the founder of the multinational fast-food chain McDonald's, put it this way:

'Nothing in the world can take the place of persistence. Talent will not; nothing is more common than unsuccessful men with talent. Genius will not; unrewarded genius is almost a proverb. Education will not; the world is full of educated derelicts. Persistence and determination alone are omnipotent'

The strap-line earlier in this Chapter from the blue chip company advertising a vacancy said it all - 'We're not interested in your qualifications - we are interested in your qualities'.

Before you call from the back, 'what did I do all those years in college for?' - please be assured that qualifications are often the key to get you in the door and will certainly gain you more interviews, but what determines your success is your attitude.

One illustration of this was the UK quiz show Mastermind. The producers probably would not like the description quiz show as it tended to be a touch more high-brow and pretentiously so. The venue was usually some august seat of learning, the invited guests were more often than not the lecturers and professors of the establishment, the introductory music had none of the razzmatazz of more down-market quiz shows. The hot seat was a leather upholstered chair under a spotlight and, as questions began, only the spot remained as the house lights dimmed. Very serious and dramatic. Even the quiz master was an alumnus from an ivy league university. The contestants were given a general knowledge round and a 'specialist subject' round - usually something off the wall like 'medieval brass-rubbing 1326 to 1395' or 'the development of water colour 1845 to 1902' - you get the drift. We, the plebs, had a chance with the general knowledge but could only sit in awe at the specialist questions and answers.

What point are you making? Patience - the point I am going to make is that some of the contestants had brains to burn. They had incredibly accurate memories and the ability to retrieve stored information instantly. They clearly would have done extremely well in school examinations with such gifts. Yet only the tiniest minority had achieved any success (as society recognises it) in life. When introducing the contestants the quiz master would ask them, Your occupation please? The answers were consistently, librarian, researcher, school master, laboratory assistant, civil servant, retired teacher, or as in the case of one memorable victor, taxi driver.

Personality is frequently the clinching factor in many selection or team building processes. From the simple, 'I just liked the guy' gut feeling to the more high-powered - after the High-D Margaret Thatcher, the choice of High-S John Major seemed very appropriate. After the High-C Richard Nixon - big, amiable, uncomplicated Gerry Ford was like a breath of fresh air. Not the brightest but physically robust, ex-footballer, a good swimmer and, in a word, something wholesome about the man. He was sent up as a rather stumbling awkward ex-footballer but, whatever the fun-poking, it was his lack of complexity in his personality which best fitted the vacated chair.

I see the value of understanding personality, but from a personal basis, I can only play the hand I am dealt!

Okay. Quite correct. You cannot change your innate personality but **you can adapt the behaviour which emanates from it.**

For example?

Take public speaking or having to deliver presentations. Most people dislike or even hate the very idea of speaking in public. If you lean more towards the Introvert Thinker, this can be a real challenge. You find a job which in many respects suits you very satisfactorily but it requires you to address groups of people from time to time. The first step in any problem-solving situation is to *identify the problem*. You acknowledge you don't like the task and neither are you much good at it. Step one. You'd be surprised how many people don't get as far as identifying step one, they charge ahead looking for a solution, e.g. 'maybe I should tell more jokes' or 'maybe I should use my arms more'. If you are not a funny person or a demonstrative one, these 'solutions' will only add to the problem. Few spectacles are more excruciating than someone trying to be funny who just cannot cut the mustard.

If you've acknowledged your problem, you can then dissect it. I get nervous. My mind panics. I mix up my cue-cards, and so on. Right! Why do I get nervous? In case I fluff my lines. Fine, practice until your lines are fluent. My mind panics. Why? In case I lose my train of thought. Learn a system where you cannot lose your train of thought (I'll show you one in just a minute). I mix up my cue-cards? Don't use cue cards. Here's an example.

When I was in the Health Club business, I became President of the then Health Club Standards Board which was a voluntary organisation set up to ensure certain standards of competency, safety, hygiene and other factors were adhered to by members. I loved being in the gym and I was a good communicator on a one-to-one basis with club members, but because fitness and slimming are always topical issues I began to be asked more and more to give talks at various venues. At first I was nervous and had A4 sheets of paper in front of me to ensure I stayed on track. Eventually I taught myself mnemonics and threw away all paper and cue-cards forever. For instance, one talk I gave was on the subject of

Seven Contributory Factors to Heart Disease

My mnemonic was **I Only Drink Saturdays And Sundays, Honest**.

I stood for Inactivity and I could talk for ten minutes on the dangers of Inactivity. How the heart being a muscle, just like any other muscle, if it is not exercised it becomes less efficient, the blood vessels begin to narrow, the overall circulatory system becomes less efficient and so forth. Then on to low calorific expenditure with a resultant gain in weight, exacerbating the situation by increasing the amount of tissue this less efficient heart has to supply. You get the drift. Right, what's next, ah yes - Only.
O for obesity. Definition of obesity - being in excess of 20 per cent overweight - i.e. if you should be 140 lbs. and you are 28 lbs. over that, you are clinically obese. The causes of obesity, the effects of obesity and so on. What's next - Diet.
D for diet - function of protein, carbohydrates, fat, vitamins, minerals etc.
S Smoking. You know the story.
A Alcohol . You know this story too.
S Stress. Uhuh.
H Heredity factor.

So with my simple acronym, I Only Drink Saturdays And Sundays, Honest, I would give a forty-five minute talk (longer if required) and never once panic about the next line. People would comment with surprise that I had spoken for an hour and never once referred to any notes. Maybe not written notes but I had my cue cards firmly, if not in my hand, fixed in my head. Now any talk I have to give, I take the major points and create an acronym or memory stack and make myself completely familiar with it. Then no notes, cue-cards, OHP acetates, or flip-charts are needed (unless to help the listener, of course). Nervousness is minimised. Panic just does not exist. Clumsiness - dropping prompts, losing your place on paper, mixing slides or cue-cards and all the risks of physical aids just do not happen. More important, you have the huge benefit of never having to lose eye-contact with your audience.

Forgive what might appear a self-indulgent account but I simply cannot offer a clearer example of overcoming a nervousness problem. This is not speculative theory - I was that nervous wreck.

To return to the point, your personality won't change but the behaviour it generates can be changed. If you know you are a High-I for example, you are naturally talkative and have, to a greater or lesser degree, all the qualities listed under INSPIRERS. One downside of being High-I is a weakness to show-off, to talk when you could be listening and perhaps appearing shallow to more contemplative types. If you take these factors onboard and identify them as the truth, then you've reached Step one - recognise the problem.

What can you do? Take a leaf from Dale Carnegie's book *How to Win Friends and Influence People* - start by asking people more questions. Don't just give your opinion, ask people theirs. And **don't** just go through the motions! When you ask a question - listen to the answer. Probe it if you have to, i.e. 'why do you say that?' or 'that's interesting, tell me more'. And again, listen to the response. You'll note the emphasised 'don't' above. I'll explain why.

Years ago, I worked with a guy who was so High-I, he was off the scale. You always heard him before you saw him. Invariably laughing, joking, flattering, embracing, encouraging - you know the adjectives. In fairness, he was a kind and generous man but too keen to be liked and generally speaking he was generally speaking. Because we were in a Training environment, the message did get across that full volume High-I didn't always win hearts and minds and that the application of a level of S or C or even some D would enhance his overall behaviour. Trouble was, he got it half right. He started asking more questions, *How are you? How was your holiday? How are the children doing at school? Is your mother still in hospital?* You know, the hundred and one questions which trip off the tongue, particularly of a High-S. A great start, but - a big but - he seldom waited for the answer or if he did wait for the answer did not dwell upon what was being said. So, with the mother in hospital being at death's door - this clearly needs a succession of sympathetic questions and some reflective silence in dealing with the answers. If you insensitively change tack with, '*apart from that, is everything okay with you*' - more damage is done than by not asking in the first place.

Lest we become too self-oriented, remember that the power of understanding personality profiles is wide. It helps us understand the behaviour of our children, our parents, our relatives, our friends, our colleagues at work, our bosses, in fact everyone with whom we have to communicate. Perhaps most importantly it gives us a common language and makes typecasting easier by affording us convenient handles to put on behavioural profiles. Forgive me for being personal again, but the golden rule in writing is write what you know about and I know about my wife. She proof reads everything I write and can spot a missed apostrophe or comma from a hundred metres (well, most of them - Ed). She is also now a very knowledgeable psychometrician. Just one brief example:

A friend of ours is a retired Mathematics Professor. A good decent man and a High-C - not surprising as a Maths Prof. His daughter was being married and he had to travel a couple of hundred miles to attend the wedding. Not long after he returned, he telephoned me to discuss a political matter as we were both activists in the same political party. My wife took the call, passed the phone to me and whispered, 'do ask him about the wedding'. Then she added, 'I bet he describes the journey.' I took the phone and began, 'tell me, how did the wedding go?' 'Ah…', he said, '…we decided to travel down the A702 instead of the M8 as we thought the traffic might be thinner and as it turned out we'd allowed four hours but managed the journey in three and a half…' Uncanny. I asked my wife later how she could be so sure. She just said he was a High-C and they all love detail and correct chronological sequence. Although I think the journey bit was sheer luck, she nonetheless had hit a behavioural bulls-eye.

Another occasion was when my wife had gained some extra weight. She determined to adopt a disciplined dietary regime. After almost three months of strict adherence to her routine, she had lost some 16 pounds. She was delighted. She looked better, felt better, had more energy and she could wear clothes which had been consigned to the No 2 drawer. In a call to her mother where one could hear her enthusiasm vibrate down the line, her mother commented, *'Now you be careful dear, don't overdo it'*, along with one or two other cautions.

These negative admonishments had a wholly deflating effect. She had expected a reaction from her own quadrant's (High-I) perspective, which of course would have been, *'Wow, great news, that's terrific, well done kid, you are just brilliant - I bet you are really pleased!'* Classic High-I enthusiasm, buoyancy and inspiration.

However, good woman that she is, mother-in-law, is not High-I but High-S (very), the quadrant which is caring, sympathetic, concerned about relationships and about people in general. Let us emphasise the point once more, her mother was not being negative - any apparent negativity was motivated out of a deep sense of care. Alas, though intrinsically good and loving, it is not what one wants to hear.

A High-C would have responded differently again. *'16 pounds, hmmm, how long did that take you? What was the dietary regime? What was your calorific intake? Did you balance it with a vitamin supplement? Were you exercising as well? ……'*

Neither enthusiastic nor cautionary but factual.

The High-D might have said, *'Well done, mind you, you were looking a bit fleshy'*. Hard, direct and, to the more vulnerable, it might appear rather unkind and insensitive. That would not be the High-D's intention. The D would simply be stating, in the D's normal assertive way, the facts. The High-C, after the analytical questions, is also quite capable of a factual appraisal, *'Yes, I thought you were looking a lot heavier when I last saw you'*.

In the wedding scenario above, The High-I, on being asked how the wedding went would have replied that it was great, what a party, what fun, went on till three in the morning, everyone awash with booze, dancing to old 60s numbers and so forth.

The High-S would say how lovely the Bride looked, loads of adjectives on the bridesmaids, the flowers, the relatives, how a tear came to the eye watching the parents doing a waltz together - you get the picture.

As for the High-D - brief, factual, never cold but direct and to the point. Good day, great party. Father did her proud. Well organised. Pastor a bit saccharine for my taste but he did a decent job. What else can I tell you?

Though my wife was disappointed at her mother's apparent lack of enthusiasm regarding her weight loss, you can imagine just how much more disappointed, angry even, she might have been had she not understood all about Four Quadrant Behaviour. She knows her mother is a High-S, yet she still feels a level of hurt and frustration at her mother's response. Consider how, day in, day out, we all convey messages to others from the perspective of our own quadrant and anticipate a response from the same personality profile. If someone with an understanding of 4QB can be disenchanted with an unappealing delivery, just how much resentment and hostility can people feel who have no grasp whatever of Personality Profiles. The High-I enthuses about a Mediterranean holiday and the High-S responds with cautions about how busy it will be at this time of year, won't it be too hot, be careful of that Legionnaire's Disease, do protect yourself from skin cancer and a few other cautions about food and drink - all motivated by concern but a real damper nonetheless.

While not diminishing the importance of understanding ourselves and maybe adapting our behaviour where necessary, the benefits of knowing what makes people in general tick are invaluable. It can reduce frustration, anger, intolerance, stress, impatience and any number of hostile feelings towards others. It can make us immeasurably better parents, managers, teachers and human beings. There are books on the market with titles like *Mastering Personality Profiling for Employment Success* which may have an appeal for the buyer but the title does not really address the subject. Worse, it implies there is some formula, some crib sheet, some key to an arcane process which once revealed will open the door to a bright future. Hopefully you are already convinced this subject is not about drawing aces from the bottom of the deck but is about a genuine life skill to make us all more rounded human beings.

4

You Say Tomahto, I Say Tomayto

All personality profiles have to steer clear of cultural differences or gender differences. Options on questionnaires should not include courses of action because people behave differently from country to country. In some countries, men are quite happy to embrace other men and kiss them on the cheek. In some Arab countries, men who are good friends can walk hand in hand. In the US, the UK and many other western societies, such behaviour hasn't really caught on yet.

Instead of actions, we have to use adjectives, because they are relative. For example Outgoing and Demonstrative are descriptive of personality but not descriptive of the associated physical actions. Eastern cultures have behaviour patterns which are much more restrained than in the West. Korean culture does not favour the expression of emotions or feelings. If a personality test asked a question,

'Do you normally:

a) Show your feelings freely - or

b) Keep your feelings to yourself?'

most Koreans would opt for the latter. This in no way means they lack emotions. Jung himself proposed that type is universal and only our means of expression vary. Anecdotally, Myers Briggs Type Indicator (MBTI) professionals working in the US commented that UK extroverts seemed initially more like US introverts. Further according to Jung-Myers theory, type is inborn and the preferences remain constant, although there may be change and development in the way they are expressed.

Adjectives are relative. Take for instance, the statement, 'I'm afraid you are getting too big for the job'. Our minds race through alternatives of visual imagery, trying to fit the statement to a picture. The statement would convey two entirely different pictures were it used in the dressing room of the jockey club or in the locker room of the Harlem Globetrotters basketball team. One might be too big at 5ft 9in while the other might be over 7ft tall. Or try, 'You are getting a little fat' - two hilariously contrasted pictures if said in the changing room of a Dior fashion show or in the Sumo wrestlers training camp.

Another risk in the compilation of personality questionnaires is the choice of the adjectives themselves, before we even think of translating them into other languages. In the English speaking world alone, words have different meaning or different shades of meaning. Are you bright? This could ask if you are lively and enthusiastic or if you are intelligent and quick on the uptake. The earlier meaning of bold was impudent or naughty (still used in Ireland), now it normally denotes bravery. My own questionnaire in Chapter Two was initially made up of single adjectives. It dawned on me that hardly anyone chose *Ebullient* in question 22, even though the remainder of the profile was High-I. Some brief research discovered that people were not too sure what ebullient meant, so they skipped it and opted for their second choice. Hence the addition of a second adjective in each question. In Persian, to Compromise someone is to severely embarrass or endanger someone, as in he was caught in a compromising position. The Persian has no positive connotation for the word. In western usage it can be quite complimentary, meaning give and take. Mediator in Persian means meddler. Kurt Waldheim, Secretary General of the UN in the 80s, flew to Iran to negotiate in the hostage crisis. On arriving at Tehran he told the media 'I have come as a mediator to work out a compromise'. Within an hour his car was stoned.

Yet another risk in compiling questionnaires is subjectivity. A High-I compiling a question might ask, 'Are you fun to be with or a party pooper?' A High-C asking the same question might put it thus, 'Are you loud, noisy and shallow or deep serious and reflective?' Both loaded with personal bias.

NATURE versus NURTURE (aka Biological Determinism & Behaviourism)

The two leading figures on personality, Carl G Jung and Sigmund Freud disagreed on this. Jung and Freud began a correspondence in 1906 when their friendship began. Jung visited Freud in Vienna in 1907 and their initial rapport was immense. Jung reports that they 'talked non-stop for thirteen hours'. Jung initially saw himself more as an acolyte and is quoted as saying 'Freud is the first man of real importance I've met. No one compares with him'. That two such powerful minds should clash is not surprising. Their friendship had ended by 1913. Perhaps there was an element of pride or stubbornness in both men but the Nature/Nurture argument in most cases will not favour either - instead it will prove to be a mixture of both nature and nurture.

Freud was more a nurture man. He argued that our personalities were formed in childhood. Jung was adamant that personality was genetic. They disagreed on several key psychological issues. Freud seemed to find a sexual root for most of our actions, even down to an infant's satisfaction at the breast. Jung dismissed this, claiming the motive was much simpler, that we all derive satisfaction from food. Another divide was in that Jung was attracted to mythology, astrology, mysticism, spiritualism, seances, mandalas and even tarot cards. Perhaps all aspects of a healthy investigative mind, but Freud was more concerned with the pragmatic, the here and now. However Freud's insistence on personality being a nurture factor is highly questionable. Certainly conditioning can profoundly influence the personality of a growing child. But the innate Jungian typing is a matter of genetics, as is right or left brain dominance, determining left or right-handedness.

There are many examples of how conditioning can influence behaviour and self-perception. A naturally High-I or High-S child brought up in a brutal, cruel and loveless environment will appear entirely different from one brought up in a diametrically opposite way. Conversely a High-C child brought up in a High-I environment full of laughter, love and physical demonstrativeness will appear quite different to other High-C personalities brought up in a more subdued style.

Apropos Freud and Jung, while much of the terminology used in defining personality is Jungian, Freud identified three aspects of the psyche as the **Id**, the **Superego** and the **Ego**. The **Id** represents human drives which are 'unsocialised' or wholly inherent. The **Superego** incorporates the moral codes of elders and the **Ego** is one's conception of oneself in relation of others.

A scientific analysis carried out by the World Health Organisation in 1997 revealed a great deal about the Nature/Nurture dichotomy. The survey was to gauge how confident teenagers felt about themselves. The survey was carried out in 26 countries. The first interesting figure to emerge was that boys in every one of the 26 countries reported feeling more confident than girls. Clearly there is a cultural bias here which is just about universal. The value of the female varies from society to society from nightmarish extremes in parts of China where female foetuses can be aborted and there have been cases of live female births being destroyed. Some Eastern cultures allow husbands to beat or mutilate their wives with relative impunity. But even in more advanced, egalitarian societies where gender-bias would appear not to exist, there are still serious discrepancies. The country with the narrowest margin between boys and girls regarding self-confidence was Latvia with Lithuania close behind. One might have predicted it might be one of the ultra-civilised countries of Scandinavia but no, ex-Soviet Union member states headed the bill. (Perhaps room for a thesis here on Communist influence on social patterns.)

The survey was carried out in 25 western European countries plus Canada. Top of the list for confident kids was Spain, with France, Germany, Sweden, Lithuania and Canada in the top ten. It would be interesting to see where the US would be placed in this league. Scotland alas, was in the bottom three along with Slovakia and Estonia. Spain topping the league was no great surprise. Spanish kids are hugged, kissed and cosseted by all from the parents through the extended family to complete strangers. Another conditioning of Spanish and most continental children is their familiarity with cafe-bar life. There is no right of passage or mystery attached to bars and restaurants. Groups of teenagers will gather at a cafe-bar, have a beer, coffee or snack and move on. The British teenager, having finally made it into the adult world, often drinks too much to make up for the years of expectancy. Witness the self-consciousness of our teenagers when handling a menu. British restaurants must be unique in displaying 'children welcome' signs. The obvious corollary from such a sign is that as a general rule they are not welcome.

The Reformation as a dividing factor

Here is a classic case of Nurture affecting self-perception. Scottish people are well educated, as affluent as many of their European neighbours, they are of Celtic or Gaelic expressive blood, they gave the world whisky, reels, jigs and some of the best foot-tapping music in the world. Although nowadays church attendance in Scotland is minimal, the effect of Calvin, Knox and a rather dour, joyless form of Presbyterianism has left its psychological mark. Certainly 16th Century Roman Catholicism was pretty rotten. It was too powerful, gross, corrupt, demanding and intolerant, as the Protestant Martyrs commemorative obelisk in St Andrews will testify.

But when the Reformers chucked out the bath water of corruption, the hierarchy of cardinals, bishops, priests and so on, the over-ornate vestments, the incense, the indulgences, the gold altar accoutrements and the whole association with gothic splendour and riches, they might, just might, have chucked out the baby as well. Almost anything associated with the expression of joy was frowned upon. (En passant, the Free Presbyterian Church of Northern Ireland recently condemned Line Dancing as sinful - in the 21st Century!). Alcohol, card-playing, dancing and almost any expression of overt enjoyment met the Kirk's disapproval. Playing cards on the Sabbath was to be in league with the devil. People who put their washing out on the Lord's Day were 'talked about'. Pubs shut firmly at 10 p.m. and could not open at all on Sunday except for the hilariously misused bona fide rule. This was a law where a traveller was entitled to alcoholic refreshment at an inn, providing he had travelled an arbitrary number of miles. A sign-in book was meant to be kept at the door to indicate the distance travelled. There existed the spectacle of a small hotel with perhaps a dozen bedrooms and a hotel bar which could cater for a couple of hundred thirsty locals all ostensibly arriving from places as far apart as Land's End to John o' Groats. These laws were scrapped in 1976 but still the chill hand of joyless religion didn't quite let go.

Even today, when the large chain stores and supermarkets are all trading on Sunday, you can buy anything you wish, apart from alcohol until midday, 12.30pm to be precise. Why? Because when the law was revised to adopt the recommendations of the Clayson Commission, as a gesture to the Church, some vestige of Sabbath Day observance was retained. The main church services are all at 11a.m. and the worshippers will not all be safely dispersed until 12.30. So churchgoer and non-churchgoer alike have to wait to buy a bottle of wine to go with Sunday lunch. Absolutely crazy, but the implication remains, that alcohol is intrinsically sinful. The irony is that while waiting till 12.30 to buy some wine for the Sunday lunch, the shopper is free to visit the nearest pub and drink him/herself into oblivion. To this day, ferries cannot run to some of the more strictly Low Church islands, playground swings could be chained up to prevent Sabbath breaking by children. Some schools demurred from erecting Christmas trees. Although an entirely secular symbol imported from Germany, it still had, for some, connotations of High-Church religious celebration.

Scottish idiom is still riddled with pessimistic cautions. When children are playing noisily, someone will warn, *There'll be tears before bedtime* or in the heat of a beautiful day, *Aye but we'll pay for it later,* or perhaps at a gathering where people are having too riotous a time, *Cheery nights make dreary morns.* The put-down attitude is known in Scotland as the *I kent his faither* syndrome, meaning - how could he achieve any level of fame or success when I knew (or was at school with) his father.

A visible facet of the Scots tradition of not showing too much exuberance or joy can be observed in the succession of brilliant but outwardly dour soccer managers Scotland produced. The granite faced brigade of Bob Paisley, Jock Stein, Matt Busby, Kenny Dalgleish or Alex Ferguson, all - even after a great victory - found it very hard to allow the big beaming grin which was in their hearts to travel as far as their lips. All these men possessed a delightful sense of humour but their nurture factor inhibited them from the expression of too much joy, especially on camera. Compare this with the highly expressive Irish managers David O'Leary or Martin O'Neill.

Certainly arrogance and too much self-assuredness can be a bad thing and a touch of humility as one of God's unworthy creations can do no harm, but the latter has pervaded the Scottish psyche for too long. Another exacerbating factor is, since the Act of Union in 1707 when the Scottish and English Parliaments united as the United Kingdom of Great Britain, the Scots tongue became subordinate to the English tongue; even God spoke in English through the King James Bible. This in turn made the Scots feel self-conscious in debate within a British context. Children could speak Scots in the playground but were force-fed English in the classroom. Mothers can still be heard correcting their children, *Don't say aye, say yes!*

Too much disapproval inhibits children and stifles their spontaneity. The Scots and the Brits in general cannot get used to American parents who constantly tell their children they love them nor can they culturally grasp the US concept that anybody can be President of the USA or the belief that you can be anything you want to be. Two kids who begin life in an identical place on the Introvert - Extrovert scale can appear to be 'poles apart' simply by conditioning. The US child who is constantly given positive affirmations will seem much more extroverted while the Scottish kid regularly given put-downs will seem more introverted yet both are latently on precisely the same rung of the same ladder.

Sir David Lane, one of Scotland's leading scientists, tipped for a Nobel Prize for his anti-cancer research at Dundee University, conceded he is struggling against pessimism and low confidence amongst his peers, where there exists an expectation of failure. He said *'It is a very different attitude in the United States'*. He spoke of the can-do attitude in the US and how success is *'all about strong teams. You have to inspire teams'*.

Britain likes to believe it has shaken off the shackles of class division but the psychological scars are still there for all to see. Their language is still awash with the heritage of a monarchical structure, royals, dukes, earls, marquises, barons, knights and the dreadful pecking order derived therefrom. You can still hear English people say, *I know my place; It's not for the likes of us* or *Don't get above your station*. Until quite recently, English pubs were divided, like first class, second class and third class railway carriages into the Lounge Bar, Saloon Bar and Public Bar and each stratum of society belonged in one section and felt uncomfortable in another.

Scotland is a slightly different case when it comes to class division. Although there exists what is known as The Scottish Cringe, there is an egalitarian dimension to it, expressed as *I may be no better than I should be but nor is anybody else*. An aristocratic accent in an English pub can still evoke the forelock-touching treatment from the landlord, whereas in a Glasgow pub, polished upper class vowel sounds are more likely to merit hostility.

Juxtapose the Scottish put-down culture towards each other alongside the American positive affirmations to their kids and there is no debate, no contest, the positive wins hands-down every time. Negativity can be so destructive particularly in the formative years. When a child pipes up with an opinion only to be checked with, *And what do you know?* in a disparaging tone, it can damage confidence, and to do it repeatedly can have a dreadful and lasting effect on self-perception.

All you need is love

An unusual statistic emerged recently that the Scots per head spent more money on Valentine Cards than anywhere else in the world. Ah! surely this completely disproves your contention that Scots are inhibited and shy about expressing emotion! Sorry, quite the reverse. It is because the Scots, or more precisely Scots men, find it so difficult to verbalise endearments and tender sentiments that they buy the largest and gaudiest cards with crimson satin hearts, bearing inscriptions which if there were a Richter scale for soppy sentimentality, would be of Krakatoa proportions. Ricky Tomlinson, the Liverpool actor and singer, when interviewed on the Parkinson Show described a time when he had served a jail sentence. He had always been quite literate and he often helped other prisoners to write home. He found that the Scots prisoners had enormous difficulty in concluding their letters with endearments. The words 'I love you' just would not come. Not the emotion but the expression of it. So sad, the most fundamental of all human emotions yet through the malign influence of nurture (even if well-intentioned), a people can be inhibited from expressing it.

So, the passion is there. The Celtic/Gaelic blood still courses through the veins. Go to a Burns Supper and count the moist eyes when the singer renders *Ae Fond Kiss* or *My Love is Like a Red Red Rose*. Attend a Hogmanay celebration when Scots sing, *Auld Lang Syne; Scots Wha Hae* or *Flower of Scotland*. You can cut the emotion with a knife. It is only conditioning which keeps the lid on it for so much of the time.

An interesting comparison is the genetically identical Irish and Scots. *Scoti* was actually the Roman name for Irish. The bloodline of both countries is a blend of Celts, Gaels, Picts, Viking, Norse, Dane and Norman with a few drops of Italian, courtesy of the Romans, who amongst other things taught us land husbandry, animal husbandry and how to wash ourselves. The Irish have an additional dash of Spanish blood from the tempest-tossed Armada of the 16th Century, part of which came ashore in the West of Ireland. The name of the village Costello, not far from Galway Bay is pure Spanish and some who came from the area have a quite Latin appearance from whence came the Gaelic term 'the black Irish.' Apart from a few drops of difference, for all intents and purposes the Celtic cousins are genetically the same.

However, while Scotland rid itself of most things Catholic (Roman and Anglo) and all the paraphernalia surrounding the High Churches, Ireland clung to the old religion with all its emotional baggage, its pomp and splendour. As one church clung to its ostentation, the other deliberately chose to be more spartan. Certainly a Catholic could not wander into a Free Presbyterian church by mistake nor could a Free Presbyterian fail to distinguish an RC cathedral High Mass for a bible reading on Harris.

The Catholic culture encouraged expression, emotion, pomp, large accomplished choirs and all the glamour RCs associate with the glorification of God. (Though why an omnipotent God should need glorification is anyone's guess). The Scots Low Churches were the diametric opposite. That, along with the Presbyterian Work Ethic produced an enormous divide between two genetically identical peoples. For the sake of perspective, a sterner work ethic is found in Japan where the word *karoshi* means death brought on by job-related exhaustion.

The Celtic creativeness and expressiveness in the Irish produced some of the greatest writers in the English speaking world, including Swift, O'Casey, Joyce, Wilde, Sheridan, Beckett, Synge, Shaw and Yeats. Not forgetting some of the moderns, Brendan Behan, Seamus Heaney, Edna O'Brien, Roddy Doyle and any number of gifted wordsmiths. Similarly the pop music firmament contains a hugely disproportionate number of Irish stars - musicians, singers, dancers, actors and comedians. Mention U2 or River Dance anywhere in the world and watch the smiles of recognition. So much for creativity in the arts but what about Irish engineers, inventors or famous financiers? Hardly any.

The equally creative Scots channelled their energies into engineering, inventions and finance. The Scots engineer became a movie cliché. Even Star Trek's engineer was called Scotty. Souvenir tea towels in Scottish gift shops usually stock the one which lists most of the Scots inventors, inevitably including Bell, Dunlop, Baird, Fleming, Macadam, the Adam brothers, Watt, Simpson, Lister and a host of others who gave us, inter alia, the telephone, the TV, the fax machine, the pneumatic tyre, the vacuum cleaner, tarmac on roads and medicines to deaden our pain, sterilise our germs and cure our diseases. Of course Scotland produced Walter Scott and RL Stevenson and some fine painters, but the creativity was channelled towards industry rather than the artistic. The classic reaction in Scotland to someone in the arts or theatre is, *Can't you get yourself a proper job?*

Tiny Northern Ireland has the same divide. Comedians, writers, musicians and actors tend to have Irish surnames (poet Seamus Heaney,

Stephen Boyd who made it big in Ben Hur, and Liam Neeson) while the more serious professionals are more likely to have Scottish names.

The Presbyterian Work Ethic

Yet another example of the Scottish conditioning regarding both industriousness and egalitarianism is the involvement of Scots in politics, especially liberal politics. The British Labour Party, from its founder Keir Hardy to the present day, has numbered a hugely disproportionate number of Scots, as did the Liberal Party. In 2001, a unique predominance of Scots was established. The Prime Minister, Tony Blair; Leader of the House (and ex-Foreign Secretary), Robin Cook; Social Security, Alistair Darling; Chancellor of the Exchequer, Gordon Brown; Head of NATO, George Robertson; Northern Ireland Secretary, John Reid; Lord Chancellor, Derry Irvine; Leader of the Liberal Party, Charles Kennedy; Father of the Liberal Party, Menzies Campbell; Leader of the Conservative Party, Ian Duncan Smith; Add to this Blair's Predecessor, John Smith; and Charles Kennedy's predecessor David Steele; along with Michael Martin, the Speaker of the House of Commons - all Scots, and the statistical improbability for a people comprising just ten per cent of the UK becomes dramatically apparent. If the UK statistics were not sufficiently striking, the fact that seventeen US Presidents were of Scots-Irish descent seals the matter. For the history student, these were Andrew Jackson (1829-37), James Knox Polk (45-49), James Buchanan (57-61), Andrew Johnson (65-69), Ulysses S. Grant (69-77), Chester Alan Arthur (81-85), Grover Cleveland (85-89 and 93-97), Benjamin Harrison (89-93), William McKinley (97-1901), Theodore Roosevelt (05-09), Woodrow Wilson (13-21), Harry Truman (49-53), Richard Nixon (69-74), Jimmy Carter (76-81), George Bush (89-93), Bill Clinton (93-2001), George W. Bush (01-)

The Irish-Irish/Scots-Irish dichotomy is, to paraphrase Shaw, two peoples united by dissimilar philosophies. Nature versus Nurture. As Jung propounded, personality type is universal so each culture would have an equal proportion of Dominants, Inspirers, Supporters and Co-ordinators. A casual observer might deduce that the Scots were predominantly High-C (&D) and the Irish High-I.(&S). For balance, it is proper to mention that Presidents Kennedy and Reagan hailed from the Irish/Irish side of the divide.

The English conditioning is different again, although England has a long history of warlike behaviour. Because of its conquests and wealth all acquired in the 19th Century, England began to rest on its laurels - it acquired affectation, ostentation, foppishness, dandyism, snobbery between old money and new money, and effete mannerisms which were a sign of sophistication, education and breeding. The English theatre followed this evolution. The earthiness of Shakespeare was eclipsed by mannered comedies or dramas about aristocratic (or at least middle class) families.

The US way in Hollywood was quite different. The frontiersman, the independent, tough, monosyllabic man of action was the model for American audiences, especially with the advent of the movies. While the Brits lauded Olivier, Gielgud, Redgrave and their ilk, America went for Wayne, Fonda, Mitchum and James Stewart.

When it came to filming the British fictional hero, James Bond, the conditioning of the British theatre made it impossible to find an English actor for the part. David Niven? - no, too much of a drawing-room smoothie. Sean Connery? - Scots of Irish extraction. George Lazenby? - Australian. Timothy Dalton ? - Welsh. Pierce Brosnan? - Irish. But surely there must be lots of English tough guys or hell-raisers who could play the part - what about Peter O'Toole? - Irish. Richard Harris? - Irish. Anthony Hopkins, Stanley Baker, Richard Burton? - all Welsh. There was Roger Moore, but he chose to play Bond more for laughs. British drama just does not go for the gung-ho tough guys, perhaps because there is no need to dramatise. The British fighting units are recognised as the finest in the world. The SAS is an international benchmark for excellence in both spearhead and covert military actions so also The Special Boat Service and The Royal Marines. Rather like the French cinema never went for the pneumatic sex goddess because they were quietly confident they were the masters of all aspect of l'amour, so with the screen image of an all-fighting, all-shooting, all-shouting hardman - it simply wasn't the way of English cinema.

The Rambo Syndrome

There is a danger in attaching too much importance to the screen imagery of celluloid heroes. John Wayne became the embodiment of the US hero to many. He was even awarded the Congressional Medal of Honour for services to the nation. All British recipients of show-biz gongs are under no illusion that the award is for services to the theatre (or cinema). Further, while virtually all of Wayne's British show biz contemporaries had seen active service during WWII, the Duke never served a day's military service nor heard a shot fired in anger. Another nurture or conditioning factor for the Brits is their dislike of super-macho Rambo parts. It is not the British way. The Brits were conditioned by blitzkriegs over London, Coventry, Clydebank and other conurbations; the Battle of Britain over English skies; food rationing; air raid shelters; blackouts; wailing sirens night after night; countless bombsites, raging infernos; V1 and V2 flying bombs; sleeping in the subway; the evacuation of their children to places of safety in the country and every family in the land was sick with worry over the several relatives on active service. Only a generation after the war, people in the UK had to contend with terrorist bombs in Guildford, Birmingham, Manchester, East London, Chelsea, Aldershot, Deal and with sickening regularity in Belfast, Derry and the most recent and most vile Omagh - to list only some.

The memory of WWI was even more painful. Hollywood's best would have been hard pressed to elicit any glamour from this conflict. Four years of virtual standstill. The utter squalor of trench warfare - damp, cold, smelly, unsanitary, confined in conditions which would have been condemned in a Victorian prison. Add to this the noise, the death of comrades and the utter terror in anticipation of the order to go 'over the top' often into a withering hail of machine gun fire. The scale of death was appalling. On the first day alone of The Battle of the Somme, fifty thousand young men were slaughtered.

These were the memories of soldiering passed down from father to son. It was also the first people's war. The national anthem was ordered to be played in theatres and other public places. Street lamps were dimmed. The Licensing Laws (Permitted Hours) were passed, shutting pubs during the day to encourage the War Effort. All geared to remind people they were at war. It worked - young men flocked to the recruiting stations throughout the UK. Hardly a family in the land was not left bereaved.

Stoicism, the stiff upper lip, calmness, resolve, patience and modesty became the typical qualities shown on British screens. The good people of the US had never been exposed to the real day to day horror of war, consequently Hollywood heroics were to many Brits so off the wall as to be funny. Errol Flynn as a GI in Objective Burma was a classic of this genre with Flynn just about winning the war single-handed. His concluding line *'now for those Damn Japs'* has to be the greatest piece of hyperbole in cinema history. US forces were not involved in the Burma Campaign and the bold Mr Flynn like Mr Wayne never saw active service either. The British hero was more the low key John Mills or Richard Todd.

It wasn't until the power of TV brought the (edited) horrors of the Vietnam war home to the American people that macho imagery waned and bloody realism brought the troops home. Even then both Wayne and mucho macho Rambo had to re-fight the war on screen to make the whole ghastly business more heroic and less unpalatable for the viewing public. Wayne's movie *The Green Berets* was a turkey and decent American people saw it for what it was.

However, with the total absence of the horrors of war on native US soil, the super heroic movie genre persisted with the likes of Stallone, Schwarzenegger and Bruce Willis, all latter day recreations of Superman. Now after the appalling Manhattan and Washington atrocities that particular genre of movie will die out. God knows how many years it might take before Hollywood will try to reinvent the indestructible superhero. A vicious irony has been produced by Sept 11th 2001 in that the Pentagon entered into talks with movie screenwriters to explore just what terrible permutations of mass murder might possibly still be in the pipeline from the minds of evil fanatics.

The Rambo syndrome was rather like Walt Disney violence. Tom could flatten Jerry on the kitchen floor with a mallet. Tom could swallow a stick of dynamite and his body would distend, his eyes would twirl and finally smoke would pour from his mouth and ears.

We laughed but we all knew that in the next frame Tom would be racing after Jerry at breakneck speed. No child was frightened. No blood was ever spilt. Pain was instant and never prolonged. Limbs were distorted but never broken or severed.

Die Hard's Bruce Willis jumping from a tower block roof while athletically retaining his grip on a rope was designed to thrill. Those thrills are now history. Seeing people actually jump from the Twin Towers of the WTC to their certain death rather than endure the baking heat and inevitable incineration of an all engulfing fire, were to most people the most chilling, horrific and heartbreaking scenes ever witnessed.

In Britain after WWII, there developed a whole generation of movies which could only be described as gentle. They included the Ealing Comedies, *Genevieve, Doctor in the House, The Lady Killers, The Blue Lamp, The Lavender Hill Mob, Dixon of Dock Green, The Man in the White Suit* and scores of others. People didn't begin to tear up their ration books till the early fifties and they wanted to look forward to a brighter, happier, gentler more peaceful future. They desperately wanted not to look back at six long years of misery, deprivation and death. The gentle comedies and light romantic movies of the 50s and 60s were like a balm to wounded souls.

Similarly, to counterbalance the Depression during the 30s in the US, there was a host of stylish movies with Fred Astaire, Ginger Rogers, Jack Buchanan and others all glamorously dressed in tuxedos, patent leather shoes, spats, gorgeous dresses and incredibly romantic backdrops. The *Buddy Can you Spare a Dime* reality could wait till people were ready to face it. Again after WWII, Hollywood made some of the best 'feel good' movies in history. Their musicals of the 40s and 50s were simply matchless including all the greats, *South Pacific, Seven Brides for Seven Brothers, Oklahoma* and, in this writer's view, the greatest of all time, *Singin' In The Rain.*

After 9/11, we all need time for the shock waves to pass. Some will heal quicker than others. Some may never heal, taking their grief to their own graves, but the Western psyche will not want to be 'entertained' by disaster movies for quite some time.

The tradition of gung-ho action in the US and the more reflective style of the Brits was apparent in the Bush/Blair attitude to Osama bin Laden. While Mr Bush revoked the 25-year-old executive order banning the CIA from assassination attempts, (allowing a shoot-on-sight impunity), Mr Blair said *'our position is that we will act in accordance with international law. This is not a video game...'* (Oct 23, 2001).

Peer group pressure

Yet another influencing factor on human behaviour is peer group pressure. During one of many 'time out' jobs, I drove a school bus where I became a keen observer of how kids interact with each other - also with adults. On their own, kids were quite open, chatty and friendly to me. Other times when I'd pick them up on the bus, I'd greet them as always, yet depending on how full the bus was, they could avoid eye contact with me and not return the greeting. It didn't take long to work out why. It was cool to be monosyllabic, to be tough guys. It was weak, particularly for boys, to be seen by others smiling and greeting someone who belonged, however tenuously, to the established order, one of *them*. The girls had fewer problems, most of them would smile and say *Hi*. Sometimes I'd walk past a boy in the street and he would wave, even telling his parents, *that's my driver.* Free of the constraints of peer group pressure he could revert to type or more simply, be himself. A survey was carried out to establish why girls consistently out-performed boys in exam results. It was found that amongst boys it was considered un-cool to be seen to be too clever or academic

Numerous experiments have been carried out in this field and most readers will be familiar with them through the medium of television. Remember the Jane Elliott experiment in prejudice? American kids were divided by eye colour. The exercise took place in 1968 but its message is just as powerful today as it was then. Elliott was motivated by the murder of Martin Luther King, to prove how destructive discrimination was. She split the kids into two groups, one of which was told that they were naturally superior to the other group. In a remarkably short period of time the 'superior' group and the 'inferior' group began to behave in accordance with their perceived status. After the point was made that we can think our way into a behaviour pattern, the teacher reversed the roles. She said that she had misled them and that group B was actually more gifted, more intelligent, and would be more successful in life. Again after a surprisingly brief period, behaviour patterns began to reverse. The 'superior' group grew in confidence, self-assurance and even arrogance poking fun at the other lesser mortals. Meanwhile the 'inferior' group became more withdrawn, and less outgoing - even their body language betrayed a lack of self-confidence.

The moral of the exercise was to teach kids how illogical racism was. In the 21st Century, we have examples where Protestant adults and young people (Group A) in Northern Ireland can line a route where Catholic children, (Group B) some as young as four, are walking to school and Group A shout obscenities, blow whistles and actually spit on Group B. Alabama or Arkansas of the middle of the last century could not have produced an uglier scene. Group B's crime? They had the temerity to walk through territory which was considered by Group A to belong to them. In India, a group of young men from a higher caste severely beat another young man of a lower caste, then killed him. His crime? His behaviour was not subservient enough towards his caste 'superiors.' 'Uppity' was the dreadful word used by white racists towards blacks in the US southern states. These Indians were all the same colour - only some psychological, artificial, imaginary hierarchy existed in the minds of the participants.

Many observers on Northern Ireland attribute, in part, the continuation of the sectarian hatred to children of different religions attending separate schools. The key word here is not religions as many would argue, the key word is separate. In any county there will be great competitiveness between schools even where there is total homogeneity across the whole range of pupils. Private school versus state school, private school versus private school, particularly on the football or rugby field.

All the pupils could come from the same type of middle-class background and all be of the same religion yet the very separateness triggered the rivalry. But where two communities are already riven by the cancer of blind bigotry, any additional separation must only exacerbate an already ugly situation.

Other experiments have established conclusively that your perception is your reality. Kids who have had it drummed into them that they will never achieve anything seldom do. Conversely, constant positive affirmations can make children (and adults for that matter) go on to achieve great success. And not just kids - Jane Elliott continued this type of experiment with adults. In the video of her work, *Blue Eyed,* we can watch grown professionals become despondent and distracted, stumbling over the simplest commands, because the inferior cap has been made fit within a period of only a few hours. To illustrate how potent bigotry can be, after her experiment was given national TV coverage, she recalls how townspeople made threatening phone calls, beat and spat at her children (Northern Ireland!) and boycotted her parents' coffee shop, eventually forcing it out of business.

You've got to be carefully taught

Remember that song from the musical South Pacific? Possibly you don't, it may have got lost in amongst all the other great numbers such as *Bali Hai, Some Enchanted Evening, I'm Going to Wash That Man Right out of my Hair* and *There is Nothing Like a Dame*. To recap - Rozanno Brazzi played the tea-planter in the South Seas who fell in love with Mitzi Gaynor. She discovers he has been married before, not only married but - shock, horror - married to a dusky native woman. The Mitzi character cannot come to terms with this because of deep-rooted, bigoted, prejudice. So she decides to wash that man right out of her hair. A fun song, but who can recall the source of her disenchantment? Brazzi, playing a Frenchman, is absolutely at a loss to understand his new love's behaviour so he confides in the young Navy Lieutenant who in turn sings him that most poignant of songs, *You've Got to be Carefully Taught. How to hate*, is the continuation of the lyric. The lyric is all the more powerful in view of the Jewish influence from Rogers and Hammerstein who needed no education on the evils of brutal bigotry. To their eternal credit, their courage prevailed and they included in their smash-hit movie a clear cut condemnation of racism - and this in the 1950s, a decade before the Civil Rights movement, Martin Luther King and the desegregation legislation which was to penetrate like a shaft of light into the darker spirit of blind and stupid prejudice.

An analogy to put prejudice into perspective can be found with animals. Someone who has several horses or dogs will not think of their colour or size but will concentrate solely on their personalities. *'This one is the most affectionate; this one is the most nervous; this one is the most obedient/stubborn/playful.'* All pet owners focus on personality. The fact that a cat or dog might be black, white, or ginger may help for identification but is an irrelevance when it comes to our feelings.

We do have to be carefully taught. Our perceptions are our reality. Sure we are all born with D, I, S or C in the ascendant so our personality preference or nature is decided early on, but in our formative years (nurture) we can have instilled into us that brown-eyed kids are superior to blue-eyed, that Protestant is superior to Catholic, that Hindu is better than Moslem, or Shiite Moslem is a truer religion than Sunni Moslem or one nation is cleverer/lazier/cleaner than another. You can choose any permutation of difference you wish. From a psychometric perspective, the most important factor of all is to be wary of assuming that one quadrant of 4QB is superior to another. Okay, maybe one may feel more at ease with a certain quadrant and be 'poles apart' with another, but every quadrant will have similar feelings and not only does that disprove any superiority but conclusively proves total equality.

But surely certain personality traits can be more valuable than others?

Only in certain circumstances. If you had to undergo brain surgery, you could be a lot happier knowing a High-C was holding the scalpel. Or if some deadly virus had to be identified and a serum found for its destruction, we might sleep easier in our beds knowing the team on the job were not all High-Is, telling each other jokes and reminiscing about last night's party. We'll be looking at Team Building later on but it is worthwhile to stress here that all traits are gifts sharing complete equality.

To return to the theme of cultural differences, we acknowledge earlier our debt to the Greeks for having a word for it. Not only the Greeks, but it would be impossible to carry on a discussion on medicine, psychology, philosophy, law, philology or science without the Greeks and Romans while many of our other idioms are derived from the French and German. Surely English has given back to Continental Europe some of its riches? H'mm, well there's always *le weekend* and what about *le hotdog* or *le parking*. Makes you proud to be an Anglophone.

Cultural differences give us received ideas or fixed ideas, better expressed by the French terms *idée fixe* and *idée reçue*. While we know Jung identified certain types, we also have fixed cultural stereotypes. National stereotypes abound and may confuse the student of psychometrics.

> A joke told by a Finn concerned two Finnish men who took crates of vodka off for a week of boozing in a remote log cabin with a sauna. After some three days of hard drinking, one Finn turned to the other and said, *'Don't you think we should maybe do something about some food?'* After brief reflection the other Finn replied, *'Have you come here to drink or to chat?'*

Jokes about nations are only of any value if they are told by the national concerned, otherwise we hear objective jokes told by other nationals, usually to disparage another ethnic group. In the US there was a preference for *Polak* jokes. Canadians developed a taste for *Newfie* jokes. Before the Berlin wall came down (and for some time after) West Germans had a nice line in East German jokes. The English seemed to produce what they called Irish jokes on a grand scale and, while some were funny, all of them contained the barb of patronising superiority. As no other nation on earth told 'Irish Jokes' it probably tells us more about the English than about the Irish.

For a joke of a national nature to be good it must encapsulate some of the real idiosyncrasies of the people, some of the true personality traits.

> A good Irish joke, told by an Irishman, described how an Irish labourer was fired from a job on a London building site by a nasty Cockney foreman. The Irishman took an Unfair Dismissal case to an Employment Tribunal. To justify his action, the foreman implied that Paddy had a low IQ and could not tell a joist from a girder. Paddy immediately piped up, 'That is not true, Joyce wrote Ulysses and Goethe wrote Faust.'

The story embodies the Irish/Celtic love of learning and literature.

> Or try the one about the American tourist in Ireland whose car breaks down in the middle of nowhere. All his attempts to re-start the car fail. Suddenly a horse puts his head over the dry stone wall, looks for a moment and says 'Check the spark plugs.' After a period of total disbelief the American does as he is bid. The car starts. Pulling into a pub a few miles further on, he buys a drink and stands shaking his head. The barman asks if anything is troubling the visitor who hesitantly tells him the tale. The barman nods and asks, 'Was it a black horse or a white horse?' 'A black one.' 'You're lucky,' says the barman, 'the white one knows nothing about cars.'

A real Irish joke portraying the love of folklore and story telling with a delight in sheer nonsense. Unlikely to be a Finnish joke.

Received ideas/idées reçues are like fashions, they change from time to time. Take the Hollywood presentation of the tough guy. In the 40s, the tough guys were men like James Cagney, Edward G Robinson, Humphrey Bogart and George Raft. No-one seemed to pay any attention whatever to their height or lack of it.

One of the classic Westerns of all time was *Shane* made in 1953. It had all the ingredients of how the US likes to see its heroes. Alan Ladd as the eponymous hero was quiet, disciplined, courteous to women, never one to start trouble but never one to run from it if it meant ducking a moral responsibility. We loved it and the issue of Ladd's diminutive stature was never raised. Alan Ladd said of himself, *'I have the face of an ageing choirboy and the build of an undernourished featherweight. If you can figure out my success on the screen, you're a better man than I'* . A remarkably honest and self-deprecating appraisal showing a sensitivity in the man. Perhaps it was this very sensitivity which brought about his untimely death not long after screen heroes had become much taller and fun was poked at how the movie sets in Shane had all to be built to four-fifths scale to allow for Ladd's shortness.

From the 50s onwards directors decided to give us more hero for our money. Big became beautiful. The six-feet-plus brigade included John Wayne, James Stewart, Gregory Peck, Cary Grant, Gary Cooper, Robert Mitchum and more latterly Clint Eastwood. It would be inconceivable to shoot a Western with the tall brigade at one end of the saloon squaring up to Cagney, Raft, Robinson and Co at the other end. More like a clip from the comedy *Blazing Saddles*. After height, the fashion was for muscles with the likes of Charles Bronson, Arnold Schwarzenegger and Sylvester Stallone.

What didn't change was personality, the same character traits we admired in Bogart, say, in *Casablanca* were carried forward to the big guys. Only the physical stature changed. We admire restraint, courage, nobility, honour, laconic well-delivered one-liners and not too much unnecessary verbiage. Japan's popular tale of heroism *The Seven Samurai* was just as popular in the west as *The Magnificent Seven.*

British heroes were different. Because of the grip of class divisiveness, tough guys never caught on for the English cinema. Perhaps the closest representation of a tough guy by an Englishman was Michael Caine in *Get Carter* but it is not the English métier.

Incidentally, it was Caine in his autobiography who said the difference between English thespians and US thespians was that the English actor looked at a script and said, *'Is this all I've got to say?'* while the American actor asked, *'Have I got to say all this?'* Caine also observed the Brits used to refer to the talkies while US actors preferred the movies, illustrating preferences for words in one and actions in the other.

Tough guys, for the Brits, carried the association of truck drivers or villains whereas the English hero had to be suave, debonair, sophisticated and have all thc bearing of the upper classes. Even some crooks and all the private dicks had to be upper class such as Raffles the gentleman thief and Private Dick Lord Peter Wimsey. Poirot never solved a case in a truckers' diner - it was invariably at a country house dinner party or on some fabulous railway train or river boat. Typical English heroes were Jack Hawkins, David Niven, Charles Dance, Nigel Havers, Trevor Howard, Richard Todd, John Mills and a host of 'officer class' stereotypes. So prevailing was the class division that senior policemen in British movies were given upper class accents which is entirely artificial as there is no 'officers and men' recruitment in the UK police force.

US stars like Fonda, Mitchum or Wayne could play a saddle tramp, a bum, an admiral or the US President without a perceptible change in accent. In *The Bridge on The River Kwai* there was a cinematic impossibility had it been in a British context. William Holden has been captured by the Japanese and is thrown into the British Officers POW camp. After a while Holden admits to his British fellow prisoners that he is an impostor. He admits to being an ordinary sailor - 'a swab jockey' is how he describes himself - and not an officer. The reason for his claiming to be an officer is because he feels he would receive better treatment from the Japanese. A British 'swab jockey' to pull off the same stunt would have had to change his accent, his mannerisms, his vocabulary and his very bearing. His brother officers would want to know who his people were, where he went to school, what clubs he belonged to and the hundred and one minor details which made up the strict social divisions extant in the 1940s.

As the Received Idea of American male hero physically changed, giving us more man for our money, so too did the image of the American heroine. Can anyone remember Katherine Hepburn or Barbara Stanwyck having breasts - or Lauren Bacall? Bette Davis we remember for her ability to dominate the screen and the power of her most eloquent eyes. Similarly with Hepburn we remember her rather imperious and slightly metallic diction. Bacall was laconic, confident and both amused and amusing. Did she have womanly hips or a big bust? Who can recall. But as the boys got bigger, so also did the girls. Jane Russell thrust herself onto the screen in *The Bandit* with the help of a movie poster showing her voluptuous curves lying in the hay. The incomparable Marilyn Monroe came after. Her sashaying evoked responses hitherto reserved for Walt Disney cartoons. Just when we thought the pneumatic figure had peaked, enter Jayne Mansfield, a woman who could give an hour glass an inferiority complex, making it feel like an egg timer. The Italians chipped in with Gina Lollobrigida and the glorious Sophia Loren. The Brits were never too happy with sex appeal but they did deliver Diana Dors. The French, as always, take sexuality like food and wine with the confident assumption they are the masters. No bulging brassiere cups for them, but they did give us the sublime Bardot, elegant, graceful and on screen, pure sexual dynamite.

Amazingly, the fashion for the more womanly figure created an advertising vogue for falsies (younger readers may have to ask mother), not just to enhance the bust line but magazines and comics of the period carried advertising for buttock and hip falsies - convex padding which could be slid inside female underwear. Can you imagine today a woman trying on a pair of jeans and asking, *'Does my bum look too small in these?'*

Should any further evidence be needed of how Received Ideas can change from country to country or generation to generation, consider the depiction of the female form in art. Eve, Venus and Diana in all their representations were big girls. Boticelli, Da Vinci, Michelangelo, Reubens and the early painters gave us the pin-ups of their era. Put them on a Baywatch set and the directors would demand, *'Would someone get rid of those fat dames'.*

Fast forward for another change - after the wonderful Holywood hour-glass era, perhaps the greatest disaster ever to strike western womanhood was Audrey Hepburn. Here was a facially very pretty woman with no breasts, no hips, and no belly, who became a fashion icon. Britain countered with Twiggy and Jean Shrimpton. How many million women put themselves through the misery of near starvation and strenuous exercise routines in a vain attempt to acquire the look. The old guard would not consider being found dead in a gym. Bette Davis would have settled for a large gin and a cigarette. Likewise the tough guy stars of the 40s. But gyms burgeoned from the 1960s to the present day, where having your personal trainer is the in thing to do.

Cultural differences exist and it is foolish to ignore them. Irrespective of whether one is a Driver, an Inspirer, a Supporter or a Co-ordinator, a knowledge of how other people's culture influences their behaviour is extremely important in any form of business exchange, negotiation or confrontation.

As a footnote to the Nature v. Nurture influences, while we accept the basic behavioural preferences are acquired genetically, we know that there are many factors which mould our personalities as we grow up through the formative years and beyond. Any psychoanalyst who wishes to understand a patient will invariably ask questions such as, *'Tell me about your childhood. Tell me about your father and your relationship with him. Your mother.... Schooling. Your interaction with brothers and sisters...'* and so on. An analyst can establish behavioural disposition through any number of psychometric tests but equally important in assessing how someone responds to the world is to establish how the world has treated the patient.

SUMMARY

Personality is the sum total of who we are and how we communicate with others. It is formed through several factors:

Genetics

Our preferences within the context of Jung's functions. Thinking-Feeling; Sensing-Intuitive; Extrovert-Introvert. Our nature.

Left brain/right brain

Will decide whether we are left-handed or right-handed. Right brain is loosely described as the creative side and left brain is the logical side. Each side controls the opposite side of the body. For example the proportion of right-brain/left-handed architects is manifestly disproportionate to the ratio of left-handed to right-handed people in general. Show business and advertising people display similar patterns.

Cultural differences

While we are all somewhere on the line between Extrovert and Introvert, the acceptability or approval of demonstrative behaviour varies from society to society. The French for example would shy away from the side-clutching, rolling-on-the-floor-with-laughter behaviour that other nationals might display. Subtlety and sophistication is more their style but they are far from lacking in humour. Witness the delicacy and charm of a Jacques Tati movie. (See also the Security Guard experiment below).

Received ideas / fixed ideas

How little boys should behave and similar rules for their sisters. Boys toys and girls toys. Boys don't cry. Little girls are made of sugar and spice and all things nice. What makes a man manly or a woman womanly. I remember running home, when I was a boy, to tell my mother that I had seen a woman bus driver. She thought I'd made a mistake. Both of us blinded by prejudice - albeit a totally innocuous one - but a form of prejudice nonetheless. Transpose that innocent narrow-mindedness to some colour or racial bigotry and it is easy to see how irrational, ignorant and blind hatreds can be developed.

One example of how fixed ideas can influence our behaviour was an experiment carried out on British TV in 2001. A civilian security guard (an actor) entered a railway carriage. Most seats were empty. One passenger sat alone at a table designed to seat four. The actor, asked the man if he could take his seat. The man folded his newspaper and quietly moved to another table seat. The 'guard' proceeded to repeat the exercise again and again. Every single person asked, quietly and obediently moved from their seat. Not one person asked, *'why do you want my seat; what's so special about my seat; who are you or explain what's going on - let alone say, 'on your way buddy, I'm quite happy where I am'*. National characteristics come into play here. The Germans might have obliged in the assumption that the man in uniform had the right of authority behind him. The Brits, being more passive and always ready to avoid making any kind of fuss might oblige as moving seat was a lesser evil than demanding to know what was going on. It would be interesting to carry out the same experiment in the USA. People conditioned by living in a spit-in-your-eye democracy in the land of the free might well say, *'Up yours Jack, this is my seat'*

Nurture

How we are brought up. The love we are given or the lack of it. The encouragement we are given. The put-downs. The affection. The cruelty. The education, the vocabulary used around us, the interest in learning which surrounds us. The thousand and one influences which mould our self-perception and how we interact with others. Using just one appalling influence - there is a high proportion of paedophiles and sex offenders who were themselves offended against.

Peer Group Pressure

Jung and Freud were both correct in that we are conditioned by a mix of Nature and Nurture. While Nature determines our base type, Nurture determines our behaviour. We looked earlier at the classroom experiment with the schoolchildren being divided into separate groups, decided by hair or eye colour and how children began to display the traits expected of them. After World War II and the Nuremberg trials, we went through a great period of soul searching. How on earth could men sink to such appalling depths of cruelty and barbarity in their treatment of their fellow men and women. How could concentration camp guards permit the awful obscenities which were carried out against the Jewish inmates? How could the Nazis have been so consistently brutal and so unflinchingly callous while inflicting the most unspeakable cruelties upon other human beings? How could these men return to their wives and families for an evening meal and not feel utter shame at the depths of their depravities. At Nuremberg, the repeated defence was, 'I was only obeying orders'. To their credit, the judges determined that a higher order existed; that we are all responsible for our actions when we transcend the bounds of common humanity and decency. When acts become so iniquitous as to offend against any norms of morality, then 'obeying orders' could not be accepted as a plea of mitigation.

However, the mystery of how people can take actions contrary to their own standards of morality and decency remains. One 1971 experiment which was well documented (and televised) was where two groups of American students and non-students (all randomly chosen) by Stanford University were separated into 'guards' and 'prisoners'. It was not long before the 'guards' showed signs of becoming distinctly autocratic and authoritative while the 'prisoners' became more submissive, subordinate and some showed signs of wishing to curry favour with the 'guards'. The participants were being paid and they knew it was an extended role play (originally scheduled for two weeks but abandoned because of the mayhem after six days). If human beings can perceptibly alter their behaviour in a simple role play, one can extrapolate from that just how susceptible people could be to change, if the roles were permanent. One of Shakespeare's many poignant lines was 'Man proud man, dressed in a little, brief authority.' (Macbeth). We have all seen this in action; the minor official who struts his stuff needing to have his petty authority acknowledged. Enough 'to make the angels weep' (to complete Shakespeare's quotation).

On a personal note I have witnessed similar behaviour patterns in the Navy. A small ship carries no NPs (navy police), so when such a ship visits a remote port, it is often required to put ashore a couple of men in NP accoutrements, (white gaiters, white webbing belt, NP wrist-band and a night stick). These are just ordinary guys from the duty watch, yet to see them patrol the harbour precinct or local bar area is to witness a distinct behavioural transformation - even to the point of not smiling or giving a friendly wave to their messmates.

One other alarming experiment carried out, again in the USA, was the 1961 Stanley Milgram experiment in an electric shock punishment scenario. A guinea pig volunteer was asked, under apparently clinical supervision and controlled conditions, to administer gradually increasing electric shocks to a 'volunteer victim' in an adjacent room. The 'victim' was in a 'learning' role, being faulted for mistakes he made. The 'teacher/torturer' could see the 'victim' through a glass panel. At each shock, the 'victim' jumped and cried out. As the current was apparently increased the 'victim' responded more violently and screamed the louder. Although the guinea pigs repeatedly voiced their concern and expressed some unhappiness as the exercise progressed, they were prepared to accept the reassurances of the 'scientist' conducting the experiment.

The exercise, *Obedience and Personal Responsibility,* where all were actors except the guinea pigs, was the product of the horrors of the Nazi regime in World War II. Sadly it did prove that even our average Joe could be capable of overriding his own sense of right and wrong with the appropriate level of persuasion. Sixty per cent of the guinea pigs obeyed orders to punish 'the learner' to the very end of the 450-volt scale! No guinea pig stopped before reaching 300 volts. One interesting if depressing question asked by the guinea pigs was who will be responsible if something goes wrong. Hence the focus was shifted from damaging a human being to who would carry the can. When reassured that all responsibility lay with the 'scientists' concerned, the guinea pigs were prepared to continue.

Physical Factors

Beautiful children normally grow into beautiful adults. Being told how attractive one is throughout one's formative years could make someone exceptionally sweet-natured, confident, relaxed in company, popular and an easy communicator. There is also the concomitant, if lesser, risk of making them a pain in the arse.

Similarly, unattractiveness may have a strong influence on personality. The strength of character of the individual will be the defining factor in the overall influence. Height can have a strong influence on behaviour, particularly for the male. There is a popular belief that shortness in stature can drive men forward with greater resolve than their taller brothers. Examples are often quoted using among others Andrew Carnegie, Napoleon, Hitler, Franco and Mussolini. Some dangerous people with a grudge against society are found to have an inadequacy of some sort or another - intellectual, sexual, height, being bullied as a kid, whatever.

Having been in the Gym business for a dozen years, my observation was that a large proportion of body-builders were driven by some form of perceived inadequacy. Interestingly, research carried out in Oct 2001 by Katherine Phillips, a psychiatrist at Brown

University in Providence, Rhode Island, seems to confirm my hunch. She describes the bodybuilders' obsession as like anorexic women, they have a distorted picture of their bodies. Men with what she terms as 'muscle dysmorphia' are worried about being thin or puny rather the fear of being fat. Despite the constant warnings about the misuse of anabolic steroids, these men are driven by 'body dysmorphic disorder' (BDD) and risk damaging their health in the pursuit of the body beautiful. My observations were less clinically specific regarding a perceived inadequacy. The motivation to work out each day for hours could be as simple as being bullied as a kid, being too short, being less gifted, having a disfigurement or a yearning to be admired - what I called a compensation factor

Stress

This is a subject which recurs throughout the book. Stress can be long-term or short-term. It can be brought about by an inability to cope or where the role requirements are too much in conflict with the natural personality or as Jung might put it - where the persona is too distant from the natural self. The persona/natural self conflict could also be classified as an inability to cope. We recognise it when we see it - actors miscast or people behaving out of character. A lie detector test is in essence a measure of short-term stress. When we tell a lie, there is an internal conflict. We have to invent, change circumstances, paint a new and false picture and we give off signals. Pulse rate and blood pressure are liable to change, sweat can be evident and detectable. A term has been coined to encompass the physiologically detectable stress we undergo when lying - it is called Biometrics. Equipment is being developed where voice analysis can detect minute changes in the speaking voice of one who is not at ease with what he or she is saying. Insurance companies have a keen interest in this development as it is estimated that the industry world-wide pays out some £17 billion in false claims.

Many wives do not need such a machine - they'll tell you confidently, *'I can always tell when he's lying'*. One indicator is said to be that our eyes travel to the side of the brain from whence the information comes. Therefore if we lie, our eyes can drift upwards and to the right (creative side) while when telling the truth but needing to recall, our eyes travel up and to the left. The stress we engender will make us give off minute body language signals which those close to us can pick up.

One memorable example of short-term stress was at the British Labour Party Conference in 2000. Prime Minister Tony Blair had won the recent election by shifting his party to the right and repeatedly calling the party New Labour. At the conference, there was a great deal of dissatisfaction in the left wing of the party and Blair's advisers told him he must put his stamp of authority on the party. So his keynote speech had to be delivered in Driver mode. Blair by nature is more in the Supporter quadrant. The resulting internal conflict was highly visible. Though an excellent speaker, his shirt became drenched in sweat. Had it been a radio broadcast, all but the most perceptive would not have noticed the stress factor.

In the Nixon/Kennedy Presidential contest, polls taken at the time showed Nixon had the edge on radio debate while Kennedy won the day on TV. What finally gave Nixon the thumbs down as the curtain fell after Watergate, was his sweaty, nervy and shifty-eyed appearance on TV when he addressed his fellow Americans.

Stuttering can be a form of stress. Ask someone so afflicted their opinion on some issue and the stutter will be evident. Ask the same person to sing a lyric from their favourite song, or recite a popular poem or maybe The Lord's Prayer and there will be no trace of a stutter. The well repeated lines come from the left brain (retentive) side, while the opinion has to be created.

All of us can undergo what is generally known as a personality change through stress or other emotional factors. In essence, the Jungian personality preferences remain but the behaviour we manifest can become quite different. One case was of Mrs Thelma Conway, a 56-year-old social worker. When her manager resigned, she became overburdened with work and the quality of care in the residential home where she worked deteriorated through lack of direction and control. Being the caring, conscientious woman she was, she worked all the harder but became extremely frustrated because no one would listen to her deep concerns about falling standards. For three years, she endured the stress but finally could take no more. Her Union (Unison) pursued her employer, Worcestershire County Council in England, because much of her life had been 'destroyed' by stress. Mrs Conway was awarded $210,000 in compensation. Quoted in the press, she said *'Normally I am a very confident, bubbly person but stress destroyed a lot of things in my life. It still upsets me when I think about what it has done to me and my family'*. The woman's self-description conveys very much an image of a High-I, almost certainly with the Supporter quadrant as close second or vice versa. Her place on the 4QB circle would probably be due South, half way between S and I. Under constant stress, her adapted style would see-saw from Extrovert to Introvert so also with her Thinking/Feeling and her Sensing/Intuitive as worry, paper-work and administration chores mounted. The influence on the adapted style would be so profound it would impinge upon her natural style and her behaviour would undergo change. Hopefully, as the memory fades, her natural style will regain its dominance but depending on the levels of stress, some people may never be - to use the well-used phrase - 'quite the same person again'.

In the case of deep trauma, people may superficially return to normal but the sub-conscious may remain 'scarred'. This may manifest itself in periodic fits of depression, painful flashbacks or more commonly in bad dreams.

Birth order

The great guru of Birth Order is Frank Sulloway, a psychologist at the University of California who spent some 25 years studying the effect it had on personality, culminating in his book, *Born to Rebel*, in 1996. In essence he states that the first born is more likely to adopt the values of the parents, including the importance of doing well at school. They also benefit in knowledge and understanding by being the focus of parental attention from their earliest years.

The second born may see the parents and elder sibling as 'the establishment' so the second born is more likely to experiment with hair dye, body piercing and generally unconventional conduct. January 2002 gave the world evidence of Sullloway's theory when the media pounced on young Prince Harry for underage drinking and smoking cannabis. Of course, the very word unconventional is a moveable feast and begs the question 'unconventional to whom?' Perhaps Harry's behaviour was unconventional to his father but on the Richter scale of wildness, smoking a joint and a boozy night out is not of seismic proportions and in view of boy's boarding school routine along with the loss of his mother, the boy seems remarkably stable.

The UK guru is Richard Woolfson, child psychologist based at in Glasgow and author of *Sibling Rivalry*. He says *'The first born generally tends to be the highest achiever, to be brighter and sharper and to do better. It doesn't matter which indicators you use - career, marriage or income - they tend to do best'*.

Of all the anecdotal evidence quoted, one statistic is quite stark - of the 23 astronauts sent into outer space, 21 were first born or only children.

Youngest siblings tend to be the most easy-going. They make good leaders and survivors having had as Woolfson puts it 'to develop basic cunning to succeed within the social group'. They know attention is not lavished upon them automatically, so they have to work that bit harder and smarter to attain positions of authority.

What about Morals and suchlike?

Many people with a strong sense of right and wrong will have acquired it through Nurture. But there are so many exceptions. Kids who had wanted for nothing may turn out to be bad people. And kids who never had an even break can aspire to be wholly decent, honest and admirable human beings. The Jungian preferences will give us no indications of how honest someone is. There are some associations - but nothing more than associations. High-Is for example are sometimes said to be more prone to sexual promiscuity. To be scrupulously fair, it is not that the Inspirers are latently more degenerate - it is simply that their preference is to be gregarious, friendly, talkative, fun-oriented and party animals. Those qualities will automatically lead the Inspirer towards socialising and company and it doesn't take a scientific analysis to predict where this behaviour pattern could lead. Sure, the High-I may be blissfully married and have no leaning whatever towards infidelity but one can deduce the latent potential. Taking the High-Is diametric opposite - amongst embezzlers, computer hackers and financial swindlers there will be a preponderance of High-Cs, not because High-Cs are more dishonest but simply because they have the mental disposition to handle complicated calculations. A High-I crook is more likely to be a con artist of the snake-oil-salesman school. Although there is more money in embezzlement, the High-I doesn't have the intellectual predisposition for it. So morals, strength of character and honour are more attributable to Nurture and very much a throw of the dice regarding Nature.

5

Practical Applications

We have traced the origins of personality profiling from five centuries BC to the present day. Hopefully, the reader should have a good grasp of the principles of Four Quadrant Behaviour and more importantly where you can be placed within the personality sphere. You will have noticed that the imagery used to describe personality involves spheres, circles and the figure four, (mandalas and horoscopes also are circular). Both the circle and the figure four have always been associated with wholeness, such as four seasons, four suits in a deck of cards, four compass points and that tower of strength that stood four-square, (Tennyson's description of Wellington). The four and the circle encompass both the earth and the human personality. Though personality descriptions use four primary points of reference, there are many degrees (90 to be geometrically precise) between each point and your personality preference may lie along that band.

But we seldom need such fine tuning. For all intents and purposes, the four primary points are all that are required to discuss the subject with a good degree of accuracy. Psychometricians will talk to each other with many allusions to such as, *he displayed typical High-I behaviour* or *she was a classic High-S, low D*. When personality profiles are literally 'borderline', we can describe someone as CD, DI, IS, or SC, reversing the order of the two letters if one quadrant is marginally superior to the other, e.g. Jack Kennedy was probably a DI, as his behaviour displayed quite a Driver profile yet also a substantial amount of Inspirer. Let us look at some applications of this science.

Being a team player

In the world of personnel recruitment, many advertisements look like they have been penned by the same person. Certain phrases seem to recur with great frequency. You know the type of thing - *must be a self-starter, able to work under pressure, results focussed, able to take ownership, inspire excellence in this company which is at the cutting edge of technology, you will be empowered to ... etc, etc* - but the one without which no ad is complete is, ***must be a team player.***

What does it mean? Perhaps in Lewis Carroll mode, it means whatever the writer wants it to mean. The image it tends to convey is of someone who is popular among colleagues, someone who will help out others and someone who will enter into the spirit of things in extra-curricular activities, a good sport, a fun person. Your image may be quite different. What is slightly worrying is that the imagery (if intended as above) is that of an Inspirer and an Inspirer is only a good team player if the personality profile required for the job is that of an Inspirer. Any quadrant can produce good team-players. It may be that some employers include the term because it now seems the norm.

What is a team? A team is any group of human beings united by a common goal or purpose. A church congregation? No, that is a group of individuals gathered together to worship their God. There is no common goal or target. Similarly a football crowd - they are there in the hope of deriving pleasure, satisfaction and excitement. The players on the pitch are a team. For example, a Rugby Union team has fifteen players. Very big, broad, heavy men in the pack of forwards, small nimble men as scrum half and fly half, taller leaner men with great acceleration as backs. Many differences, many individual skills and differing personalities, yet all united with fierce determination to overcome the opposition and win the game.

A less obvious choice might be a huge disparate organisation such as the military. The military will comprise the four quadrants not only in personality but in functionality. The top brass will represent the Driver. They decide the plan and deliver it to the executive officers or heads of departments. These are the Inspirers, who have to pass the orders on to the troops, motivate them, secure their loyalty and their zeal. The Supporter function is filled by the supply team, the medics and the overall logistic planning. The Co-ordinator function is manifest in the technical experts, the communication staff, the computer people, the weapons systems technicians, the electricians, missile and radar experts. Jung's Four Functions are all there - the totality of any dynamic.

This of course does not mean that the top brass are all from the Driver quadrant, nor does it mean that all the technical experts are from the Co-ordinator quadrant. Certainly there will be significant representation of the matching quadrant in the appropriate role but the illustration is simply to show that in any dynamic, the principle of the four quadrants applies. During twelve years Navy service, I worked with skippers from all quadrants, though predictably the DC (or CD) was the more common.

The same principle applies in any organisation. The large multinational company will have a significant presence of Drivers in the boardroom. The Inspirers will figure quite prominently among sales managers and other heads of departments and Supporters will be present among the personnel department and the secretarial staff. Co-ordinators keep every one else in order, running the stores, the accounts, mending the computers. Any quadrant can work in any role but when the function of the job is too far removed from the personality disposition of the person holding the position, stress may develop. Conversely, the nearer the personality to the requirements of the job function, the greater the contentment of the employee.

One example of the latter is in the field of training, especially sales training. Some sales trainers are excellent at their job. They enjoy it and find it fulfilling. Their enthusiasm is infectious and they not only help to educate salespeople in their profession but inspire and motivate them to do the job. Delegates on courses often believe that the trainer must have been a top salesperson him- or herself. More often than not, this is not the case. Because the personality of the trainer matches very closely the requirements of an effective trainer, this does not mean he or she had the personality to meet the requirements of a successful salesperson. Sales trainers are often High-I. Inspirers often suffer from the please-love-me syndrome and anyone knowledgeable about sales knows that rejection rates are very high. In financial services and office equipment sales, for example, rejection rates were 99:1. Inspirers seldom can take that level of rejection. George Bernard Shaw put it more succinctly - *He who can does - he who cannot, teaches.* For balance, in the field of training there exist High-Cs who have a mastery of their subject yet lack that inspirational touch to convey their knowledge. Dominant trainers might be a tad too impatient with slower delegates and Supporter trainers might tend to spend too long with the lame duck thus holding back class progress.

To return to the *team player* term. Does the employer appreciate that teams can be formed for different purposes? Two clear divisions are:

The specific or focused team	***The all-rounder or balanced team***

A **specific or focused team** is one made up of similar personality types brought together to focus on a specific task most suited to their gifts. Research work in a lab or extremely thorough and detailed police work where evidence has to be sifted through a fine-tooth comb will suit people who are capable of long, uninterrupted concentration. These people will very likely be drawn from the Co-ordinator quadrant. Not only would the High-I (however intelligent) be unsuitable but the Inspirer's presence could have the added disadvantage of distracting the other team members. Ironically, the Inspirer, to some, matches the definition of a good team player but, no sir, not in the above scenario.

Focused teams might be Butlin's Holiday Camp Redcoats whose focus was to jolly the campers along with fun and games. The popular habit of campers tossing the Redcoat in the swimming pool might not be so well received by a High-D with a fiery temper on a short fuse. Easijet, the discount airline, seems to attract a large volume of High-I cabin crew.

Police or military squads mustered to carry out dangerous 'snatch' or 'bust' exercises are more likely to be High-Ds. This does not mean that a special regiment such as the SAS is made up of High-Ds. These special service men often have to take long undercover roles which involve extensive planning and detailed execution, so there will be an appropriate representation from all quadrants. A hostage rescue task might be a High-D operation. The hostages have to understand an order immediately - no questions and answers, just sheer overwhelming action.

A team of hospital doctors and nurses will have a higher proportion of Supporters and, in the case of surgeons perhaps more Co-ordinators. A focused team could comprise any quadrant where a certain singularity of purpose was required. After a disaster of some form, a team of counsellors might be needed to help people through some dreadful trauma. It would probably be a High-S team. The Driver might have a leaning towards the pull-yourself-together school of sympathy. The Inspirer could possibly use the cheer-up approach and try to lighten the darkness with optimism and lightheartedness. Though helpful, in the early stages of trauma or grief, this approach is too premature. People need comfort and time. The Co-ordinator might want to establish too many details - what happened, where, when, how - details can wait.

My wife and I were involved in a car smash, just before Christmas. We were struck by a macho 4 x 4 with a bull bar which city men tend to buy for effect when often they (and their less enthusiastic wives) are lacking the appropriate driving skills. The ambulance crew who took us to hospital and looked after us (fortunately nothing serious) could not have been more supportive. Not one question did they ask about cars, road conditions, speed, culpability or any of the myriad queries we all have in such situations. They only showed concern for our well-being and comfort. Wholehearted Supporter behaviour. This may sound a little critical of other quadrants but that is not the intention. Sure, the Driver who is intelligent and perceptive can adapt a forceful personality to that of a Supporter role, but the point is that Personality Profiles identify our **behavioural preferences**. So while all quadrants can adapt to the Supporter role, it is not unreasonable to assume that the natural Supporter will fill the role more effectively and sustain that behaviour for however long it takes.

A **balanced team** is quite different from a focused team. A focused team might be assembled for a specific task such as the WWII code breaking team who devoted their considerable brainpower to cracking the Enigma enciphering machine. Anyone trained in naval cryptography using the successor to the Enigma, the KL7, will vouch for the almost infinite permutations of letter substitutions which take place inside this machine. Each depression of a key triggers off a set of revolving discs (changed daily) which electronically convert by random selection of millions to one, any character into another. The single-mindedness and power of concentration required for the task of deciphering this jumble is quite awesome. This would have been predominantly a High-C team. (En passant, the movie portrayal of Uncle Sam busting the Enigma code is about as accurate as Errol Flynn winning the Burma campaign).

As the name suggests, a balanced team would involve two or more quadrants. Take an expedition of explorers or mountain climbers. The leader might be a Driver who makes the decisions, gives the orders and wants to get on with the action. The Inspirer wants to encourage, enthuse and motivate the team. The Supporter would have the role of making sure no-one was unwell or had a problem which might affect the morale or well-being of the mission and the Co-ordinator would be the only one to have checked the cans of beans, the amount of water, the toilet paper and the other essential provisions. A Co-ordinator would also have read the map, studied the weather forecast and ensured all the correct people were properly briefed.

Too many Drivers could disrupt the mission through disagreements and shouting matches. An all-Inspirer mission might be too busy enthusing, having a laugh and making light of the task. Details might get overlooked. The danger of all Supporters is that while everyone is caring for one another, they might find reasons to postpone the mission or fall into that negative mode which is not intentionally obstructive but is born of concern. Should they all be Co-ordinators, we could guarantee that the rations have all been distributed to the exact calorie, the map co-ordinates would be precise, the weather checked and so on, but time could be lost waiting for someone to be decisive and give the order to move out.

At the risk of repetition, this is not to say that no other quadrant is capable of the definitive tasks outlined. The above is a typical scenario and the nearer your role is to your personality preferences, the more effective a performer you are. Conversely, the more diametrically opposite your role is to your natural self, the greater the potential for stress and consequently a potentially poorer performance.

There's no business like show business

There is no business like theatre or cinema to convey how personalities interact. It is also an extremely useful medium for drawing examples and illustrations. You can be told about the maths professor who attended his daughter's wedding and began his account of it by describing the car journey. But though an amusing and perfectly true tale, you don't know the man. 'My uncle John is a typical Driver', is only of any relevance to those who know uncle John. However most people have seen a great number of movies, so using characters from the screen and their interaction with other characters is a universal tool for description.

Dramatists have always been fascinated by character interaction and personality balance. Many dramatists have used diametric opposites in their plays to heighten the sense of drama, yet they may know nothing whatever about psychometrics - they just have an instinctive feel for what makes good theatre. Perfectly balanced casts will often create great theatre. Opposites of any form work. The good guy in the white Stetson riding a white horse (if we failed to get the first message) was invariably cast against the bad guy in black. The *Taming of the Shrew* gave us the firebrand, spit-in-your-eye woman who eventually becomes the meek, loving and pacific wife. Shakespeare knew a thing or two about opposites, though not much about political correctness.

Perhaps the definitive, and for many the funniest, screen play on opposites was Neil Simon's *The Odd Couple*. The movie, with Walter

Matthau and Jack Lemmon as the eponymous characters, was a smash hit producing a TV spin-off with Jack Klugman and Tony Randall. Whether Neil Simon had knowledge of personality types matters not. He hit a perfect bull's eye with his characterisation. The subtlety of the movie was that it avoided what might have been predictable - a twosome who were High-D and High-S respectively. This would have been more clumsy and perhaps too easy to deliver - a Dominant, Driver opposite a Sympathetic Supporter. What Simon produced was the DI Oscar and the SC Felix. Still diametric opposites but both straddling two sides of the Extrovert and Introvert hemispheres. Oscar was a Driving Inspirer (or if you prefer an Inspiring Driver). He was forceful, assertive, abrupt yet he sought company, enjoyed a laugh and liked to party. Felix displayed lots of S - he cared deeply (too deeply perhaps) about relationships, he was emotional and sympathetic, yet he was very precise, tidy, organised and thorough - a Supporting Co-ordinator (or Co-ordinating Supporter).

To recap the theme. Felix has split from his wife and is in the depths of misery, prone to weeping and self-pity. Oscar is divorced and enjoys his rather slobby bachelor lifestyle with no-one to nag him about time-keeping, tidiness or his undomesticated habits. In a fit of largesse, Oscar invites Felix to stay with him in his apartment.

One scene said it all. Oscar, the sports reporter, is in the press box at the ball game. Felix calls him from the apartment. Oscar, with half a mind on the game and half devoted to Felix, asks why the call. Felix reminds Oscar that he said he'd be home for dinner. Oscar asks, so what? Felix reminds him they agreed 7.30. Oscar repeats, yeah, so what? Felix laboriously points out that he has been preparing dinner all afternoon and that it is now ready to eat. Oscar pauses and looks at the phone, his expression saying it all. He had just divorced himself from all this - in his mind - domestic trivia. To Felix, of course, this was unpardonable, unpunctual, uncaring and contrary behaviour - contrary, in fact, to S and C standards of behaviour.

One other fine exemplar of character definition in this excellent screenplay was when Oscar invites to dinner the Pigeon sisters who live in an apartment in the same block. Oscar, in the memorable phrase, says he needs 'to get hold of something soft'. Felix has reservations because of his relationship with his estranged wife. Oscar wants to party but Felix's emotional side gets the better of him and he ends up pouring his heart out to the Pigeon sisters, who themselves are very supportive and spend their time comforting the weeping Felix. This High-S behaviour is greeted with deep but restrained irritation by the High-D in Oscar along with the frustration which his Inspirer feels at not being able to party.

Sure the acting and the screenplay were superlatively good but it was the characterisation which afforded the movie such enormous popularity and audience identification. All four quadrants were embodied within the players. Who does not know a Driver Oscar who leaves plates in the sink and makes sandwiches with the finesse of a bricklayer. Who has not undergone the anticipation of the Inspirer Oscar waiting to greet the Pigeon sisters in the expectation of a night of pleasure. Who can not identify with the heartbreak of Supporter Felix's bust relationship. And, at the risk of being sexist, how many wives and mothers shared the hurt of Felix's unappreciated precision in the kitchen. Good acting aside, should further proof be needed of the sheer dynamic of the contrasting roles, the fact that Klugman and Randall could make a series out of the two characters say it all.

Talking with others who understand Personality Typing often throws up personal favourites where 4QB has been evident. A highly popular TV series which portrayed clearly the four quadrants was *The Golden Girls*. On the surface, the show didn't seem to have a lot going for it. Four mature women sharing a home. No outside camera, all studio produced, no beaches or stunning scenery, no violence, no car chases, no swearing, no acres of exposed flesh, no titillation - in fact, no sex at all and no guns. How could such a series work? How could it be sold to foreign language buyers? In two words, identifiable characterisation. Dorothy filled the Driver role, she was the more dominant and authoritative figure. Blanche just loved to party and had Inspirer oozing from her playful eyes. Rose could not have been more gentle, caring and sympathetic - pure Supporter and the cunning, observant and detached mother of Dorothy filled the remaining empty quadrant. Here was personality balance and whether in the US, the UK or any of the foreign language countries which bought the series, all could identify with the balance.

Pick your own - it makes for great dinner party persiflage. Trevor Howard's very High-D Captain Bligh and Marlon Brando's Fletcher Christian were the stuff cinema is made of. Okay, brilliant acting and wonderful locations, but many a movie has had these assets and turned out to be a real turkey. Brando, struggling with his background and training as a Naval Officer (his adapted style) until his compassionate and humanitarian natural style could take no more, was a cinematic tour de force.

Even the old gangster movies often embodied 4QB with The Boss (D), Brains (C), the gangster's moll or the priest, (S) and usually a gang member for light relief (I).

On stage or screen, we all recognise good character balance, good casting or when someone is badly miscast. Some have to work harder than others. Once John Wayne became a star, he continued his career simply playing himself. Whether a cowboy, a cop or a general, he seldom changed his style, his mannerisms, his voice or his walk. He would have been comfortable with that and so was his audience. His roles were always pretty close to his natural personality, therefore there were none of the problems of miscasting or as the saying goes, acting out of character. One reason Sean Connery was the most convincing Bond was because he had been a competent footballer (as was Wayne), a good boxer and he was used to working out, so he could convey a sufficient level of menace.

Great actors as Matthau and Lemmon were, *The Odd Couple* would not have worked so well had they swapped roles. We felt instinctively that the characters portrayed were closer to the personalities of the actors involved than the other way round.

Any real-life examples?

This can be difficult. The reason cinema and theatre are so useful in illustrating behaviour patterns is that we have the facility for universal focus - well amongst the movie and theatre-going public anyway. Few real-life individuals have such universal recognition, hence the illustrations in this book have included US Presidents, UK and French Prime Ministers and a few others. Even here we are limited because Heads of State are often in their middle years or above before they appear on the world stage. So all we can see is what we are shown. We have little idea of their formative years, their family lives, their natural style contrasted with their adapted style or any of the intimate data which make up a human being.

Perhaps one exception to this is the British royal family. From birth, their lives have been examined under a microscope by the media, biographers, royal watchers and other commentators. One is reluctant to make observations about other human beings but this family is wholly inured to such treatment.

Using the tools of personality profiling where would we place Prince Charles on the 4QB circle? We know every personality profile is a combination of nature and nurture. Let us look at nature first. Is he,

D? He would need to have some D in his make up or he would recoil at the thought of being head of state (as did King George VI). But it certainly is not his major suit. He displays very little of the authoritative, dominant, assertive or aggressive qualities of the D.

I? More of this to be seen. He enjoys a laugh and delivers a good speech, especially on a theme close to his heart. He was also a fan of that zany and surreal radio comedy, *The Goon Show*.

S? This is more like it. A lot of Supporter evident here. Caring, concerned about the environment, a bit of a tree hugger. Into good causes. Decent. (But what about Diana? - I was afraid that would come up - we're trying to stick to personality traits here. Don't infidelity and the consequent infliction of pain come into this? - Oh all right but in just a moment.)

C? Some C evident here. Can be a bit reclusive, introverted and analytical but anyone who enthused about *The Goon Show* would have minimal amounts of C.

He is clearly in Jung's Feeling hemisphere. Feelers are either S or I or of course, SI. Often the quickest way to place someone in a quadrant is not to follow the most like path but to begin with a least-like analysis. We established earlier that least-like questions are the easiest to answer. Least like leads us very quickly to the D quadrant. There is very little Driver in the man. compare him to his High-D father. So by logical extrapolation if he is least like a D he must be most like its diametric opposite, an S. His profile would probably read SICD.

So much for nature, what about nurture. Here's where the problems begin. His father is High-D, assertive, blunt, outspoken, dominant, often tactless in public (witness his many gaffes including allusions to slitty-eyed Orientals and drunken Highlanders, to name but two). A D father and an S son are an accident waiting to happen. In this instance as in so many others the father wants to make 'a man' of the son. It is a form of self-delusion, what the father really wants is to make the son more like he is. Anyone of intelligence accepts that this cannot be. However the father persevered. Charles was sent to Gordonstoun, an outward-bound type school in Scotland where boys were occupied daily in 'manly' pursuits. This sensitive and gentle boy must have been utterly miserable. Even when allowed home, the likelihood was the boy's mother was off on some royal visit. One of the saddest photographs of the billions taken of this family was when the Queen and Prince Philip had returned from some royal trip and the press showed the Queen shaking hands with her bewildered son. compare this with the demonstrative hugs Diana lavished on her sons.

After the bleak wilds of Scotland, Charles was packed off to Australia to continue his education. Education completed - what next? While the young man had the personality disposition to be a country parson, this is not the way for British royals. It had to be the Armed Forces. Royals do not join the Air Force as it is seen as too new and not sufficiently steeped in august tradition. The Army? This presents another problem. Which regiment, an English one, Welsh, Scottish, Highland or Lowland, the Guards etc? Patronage cannot be seen to be partisan. So it has to be the Navy. Every force of nurture was applied - pilot courses, paratrooper courses, the poor lad was dizzy with macho activity. Charles' brothers had to follow suit; no great problem for Andrew as a jolly High-I. But Edward! Here the mind boggles. Edward was the least macho of the boys. It was glaringly obvious that his interests lay in the arts, in theatre and the more aesthetic elements of humanity. Where did his High-D father arrange for him to serve? With the toughest of the tough - the Royal Marines! To anyone with the merest grasp of psychometrics or anyone who has served in the Armed Forces, more especially the Navy, here was an example of the most crass ineptitude possible. For an average family to make such a disastrous mistake would be reprehensible but for a family with all the wealth and so many of the finest doctors, psychiatrists and the best brains in the country at their beck and call to make such an appalling error of judgement smacks of being wilfully punitive. Predictably, the boy only lasted a few weeks before his High-S soul rebelled against the High-D regime. This is not a criticism of the regime, it is a clarion call warning of the dangers of putting square pegs into round holes.

The effect of nurture on Charles is manifest today as the man approaches his sixties. The wholly unintelligent determination to change the boy's personality into something other than what it was inherently destined to be has left its mark. Students of body language use clips of Charles to illustrate a range of mannerisms which display insecurity and a lack of confidence. The poor man cannot walk into a public arena without reaching for his shirt cuffs or cuff links. Either that or his hand will dart for his pocket or he will straighten his already flawless tie. His tie-knot is always of the tiny pinched variety once favoured by the British aristocracy. Not for him the large expansive Windsor knots invented by his debonair ancestor Edward VIII. When Charles attended his son's first day at St Andrew's University, William looked so normal in jeans, sweater and open-necked shirt. His father, still carrying the burdens of repression, wore light chinos, a double-breasted jacket, shirt and the unvarying strangulating tie. Charles actually looks his best in a kilt and an open-necked shirt. If someone looks good in an outfit, it is a safe assumption that they feel good. But Charles' nurture often overwhelms his nature. To see Charles in the uniform of the aristocrats who wintered at Cannes in the 1920s alongside his very normal son only highlighted his complex persona.

He comes across as such a basically decent guy, so that you want to give him a bear hug, take him to a normal pub and get down to some serious talking and drinking.

Ahem - what about Diana?

It is more the job of the clergyman or the philosopher to comment on issues of immorality, infidelity or sin. A psychometrician can only speculate on the personality make-up which may trigger behaviour patterns. However, it is not unreasonable to suspect that the root cause of this historic split was the simple fact that Charles was not in love with his wife. She was the product of a lengthy trawl by myriad Palace advisers.

The Establishment needed someone young, preferably pretty, fertile, healthy, scandal-free (virginal if possible), non-Roman Catholic, not too intelligent lest she eclipse the future monarch, of aristocratic lineage but not so close as to create risk for the progeny, plus a couple of other prerequisites. What about love? Not all that important, old boy; as long as she can produce an heir and a spare, he can always find comfort in the traditional royal style. The innately honest Charles gave the game away in an 'engagement' interview, when asked if he loved Diana, he replied 'Yes, whatever love means.' That was the root cause. But surely any man would rush to be beside such a lovely young woman? Point taken, but Charles was not 'any man'.

Sure they were both Jung's Feelers and had much in common and - saddest of all - she loved him but, where many men would love to throw a protective and guiding arm around this vulnerable young girl, Charles himself was still very vulnerable. Witness his wedding day, when on the balcony of Buckingham Palace, this man in his thirties had to turn to his mother to ask if it was all right to kiss the bride. Such insecurity is pitiful. Diana needed guidance and massive support from a (possibly High-D) man to help her through the Machiavellian workings of the royal household and all the stilted, dysfunctional behaviour. Charles needed all the hugs and kisses and mothering that he was denied as a boy.

Charles' mistress, Camilla, gave him what he needed. She was very much the mature woman whose shoulder he could metaphorically (and perhaps literally) cry upon. Diana's enormous emotional turmoil lay in her terrible dilemma - the one man she depended upon to give her support, love, warmth and comfort in this alien and austere household, was giving it to and, more importantly, receiving it from another woman. Charles found it difficult to give those emotional crutches which he sought for himself. This was again manifest in Charles' rather touching attachment to that dreadful and shameless charlatan Laurens Van Der Post, a self-invented philosopher who was at best a charming con man. The obsequious and social climbing Van Der Post appeared to give Charles some of the comfort, wisdom and paternal guidance of which Prince Philip was incapable.

Regarding Diana's own adapted style, it is to her enormous credit that, faced with such all encompassing frigidity and even hostility, she determined to survive and do it her own way. She lavished her love on her sons - it shows - and she went on from an insecure teenager to being a beautiful, confident, caring celebrity. The star of the very family who treated her so negligently.

Certainly an appraisal of real-life situations adds a greater element of drama, even sensationalism to the subject but observations of a personal nature are not desirable and were the members of the above family not so universally known and their lives scrutinised in such minute detail, one would not make further intrusions

Team building examined

At the risk of upsetting some of today's management gurus, it is important to stress that the team - or team building - is not the be-all and end-all of a working dynamic. Shock, horror, came the cry from those who have adopted the buzz word as gospel. UK TV viewers will be familiar with the show *Drop The Dead Donkey* about a TV newsroom crew. The boss, Gus, used all the modern buzz words available in the lexicon of contemporary business. Gus was incapable of saying '*step into my office I want to talk to you*' - no, it had to be, '*John, my team partner, could you join me in my work station for a one-to-one interface'*. Or *'I hear what you say; I have a window in my diary (or white space); run that by me again...'* - all the latest jargon was employed and enjoyed by Gus.

Gus would have attached inordinate value to being 'a team player'. Sure, team spirit should not be devalued but it must be viewed in perspective or within the context of a working dynamic.

The post war years produced a clutch of management gurus including inter alia, Maslow, McGregor, Hertzberg and John Adair. Adair argued that there was not one element to a working dynamic but three. These three elements had to operate in harmony for a working dynamic to be successful. He identified the three factors as:

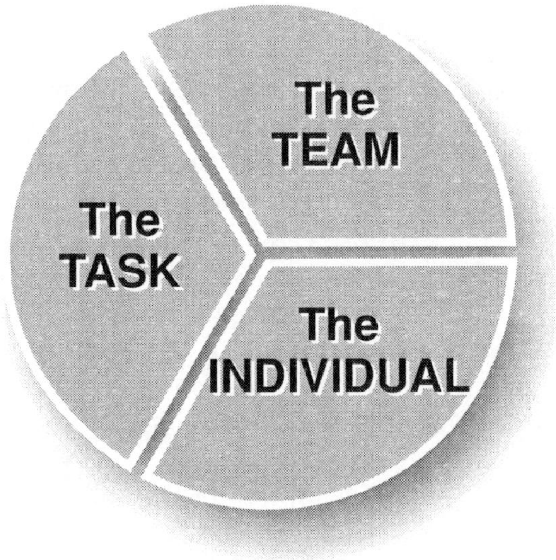

Adair would have supported the emphasis on team spirit as would any organisation from industry to the military, but he would have strenuously disagreed with viewing the Team in isolation. All three factors have to be given equal stress.

From the Industrial Revolution to World War II, nobody gave a damn about the Individual. The entire emphasis was Task, Task and more Task. The dark satanic mills which lit up the night sky and polluted the air cared little for the human misery they created. Shifts were of 12 or 14 hours. Men, women and children were all entirely task driven. Statutory holiday pay or sick pay were unheard of. The weekend, which now can begin at lunchtime on a Friday, meant Sunday - and just Sunday. There were no welfare benefits and if you did not work you did not eat. Factories, mines, typing pools, shipyards and labour as a whole were all task driven.

In the Clyde shipyards, smoking was prevented where possible on the premise that a man could not smoke and work at the same time. Men arriving at the time-keeper's window a few seconds late would have the window slammed in their faces and lose a day's pay. Breaks were not allowed though men would surreptitiously line up their billy-cans to be boiled by an acetylene torch. Should one of the management uncover the unofficial break, he would kick over the cans, often into the sea.

The Depressions in the UK and the US in the twenties and thirties showed just how appalling working conditions had been and how totally dependent people were on these very conditions to survive.

After WWII, came the acknowledgement that the Individual mattered, not only from a humanitarian and compassionate perspective but that it actually made good management sense to have employees who felt a sense of ownership or pride in their tasks. Maslow, as we have seen, propounded that man lived not by bread alone but he had a hierarchy of needs from the physiological to the psychological. McGregor identified two management styles, the X and the Y. The X was the task-driven assumption that all workers were lazy, unreliable and not worth communicating with. Make them clock-in, give them specific tasks to be carried out in a specific way and keep monitoring them to ensure they did not slacken. Hire overseers and foremen to observe every move, monitor any breaks or lavatory visits. The Y style was a management by objectives style which allowed the employee a level of initiative where his or her own common sense, intelligence or creative ability would be utilised to tackle the objective as best they could.

As the emphasis on the Task lessened, the importance of the Individual grew. Employees were given better facilities - holidays, sick pay, canteens, health checks, miners were provided with pit-head showers, trade unions could sit down with management and discuss wage rates, working hours, overtime and all the standard working conditions we now take for granted. One aspect of the Individual's importance was where the interview process involved the applicant's spouse, in the belief that a good marriage predisposed the worker to a better attitude and performance.

Working in the coach tour industry as a driver and guide, exposed some depressing pre-war-type practices. My involvement was seasonal and it suited me but the career professionals endured a great deal of old X-style management practices. Tony Blair's New Labour did introduce a minimum wage but although it was a start it was pitched far too low. An hourly minimum rate of £4.00 for people aged 22 or over; £3.50 if under 22 and no safety net whatever if under the age of 18. The European commission recommendation for the 'threshold of decency' was £7 an hour. Some companies paid rates of £4.50 an hour to its drivers. These men and women are professionals. They undergo an extensive theory examination including all aspects of heavy vehicle legislation, they are required to take a medical check-up and then they make the Passenger Carrying Vehicle practical test on the road. Just one 'major' fault (e.g. tyre over the kerb) and instant failure. Some companies will not take a driver of under three years PCV experience - so gaining that experience is made all the more difficult. To be paid £4.50 an hour for such responsibilities is wholly inadequate.

Because of the old style X-Theory working practices in the industry, drivers may accept the rate and often put in 70 or 80 hour weeks to make up a decent wage packet. Worse, they may even collude with the employer to break the very tachograph laws they have been examined on to achieve the requisite hours. Another archaic X-Theory practice, particularly common in the West of Scotland, is 'Lying Time'. This is the practice of withholding a first week's wage packet and only paying the second and subsequent weeks. Real old-fashioned X-Theory distrust of the employee lest he or she leaves without giving proper notice or in some way incurs costs to the employer. This can also be applied to holiday pay which in some companies is only paid after 12 consecutive months' work. Another nasty distrust of the employee.

Often it is not the 'boss' class who is so hard on the workers, but working class bosses made good, and their middle managers. *'When I was a lad, I never had a Saturday off/any training/holiday pay...'* is a common stonewall approach. The X-style of management is perpetuated by the low wages and long hours some people have to work.

Perhaps other drivers are too dependent on the work to risk rocking the boat. Yet another facet of X-Theory meanness is that whereas drivers may average a 65-hour week throughout the year, their holiday pay is paid on the basis of a 40-hour week at the basic rate of £4.50 an hour. This is commensurate with a salary of £9,000 per annum, while the average wage for a skilled worker is £20,000. McGregor would have had something to say about companies using such practices 50 years after he faulted them. John Adair would have highlighted the dangers of all Task and no concern for Team and Individual.

A sociological consequence of such bad practices was the serious health problems so many drivers suffer from. In a pool of eight in one tour company, one man had angina and was de-barred from lifting all but the lightest luggage, one was taking Warfarin, a blood thinning drug to prevent thrombosis, two had diabetes, and one had already experienced two heart attacks. It was not just the stress and long sedentary hours; all of them smoked; all of them had a dreadful diet of meat pies, chips, greasy food and sugary drinks (except the diabetics) and five of the eight were clinically obese. Bus driver's belly is accepted like tennis elbow.

One risk of getting too far away from the coal-face is that one adopts all the middle-class values. Working as a consultant, one is likely only ever to speak with the management, to involve oneself in their concerns and to see the world from their viewpoint. Hospitality, lunch and standards of managerial comfort become the norm, productivity can become formulaic. Even time and motion observers who spent days on the factory floor could see the workers as 'them' and just how can 'we' get more out of 'them'.

Certainly, conditions have improved enormously from the dark, pre-war days. The whole approach to work and the work place was transformed. The Task driven mind-set of pre-war years shifted to much greater concern for the Individual. For the last couple of decades, the buzz word has become not the Task, nor the Individual but the Team. To understand the value of the three elements it is necessary to examine the three working in harmony and then working in disharmony where too much or too little emphasis is placed on any one of the three.

Twelve O'clock High

One of the better examples of the three elements working in disharmony was in a post war movie titled, *Twelve O'clock High.* As the credits roll on the movie we learn that no less a man than John Adair was a consultant adviser in the human interaction of the movie. The story is a relatively simple one. It is the tale of a USAF squadron based in England during World War II. The TTI composition was as follows, the Task is to fly bombing raids over Germany and occupied Europe. The Team is the group of pilots and their CO who have to accomplish these missions and the Individual is each human being and his specific needs and wants.

The CO is probably what would nowadays be called a great team player. He cares about his men deeply, constantly establishing if they have had enough food and rest even to the point of stopping them flying missions if he considered it detrimental to their physical welfare. All very humane and civilised. However, the point Adair makes in the movie is that here the *esprit de corps* or Team is in good heart and the Individual feels valued but the problem is that the Task is not being accomplished because too much emphasis is being placed on the other two elements.

Then the CO is replaced. The door darkens and in walks the substantial figure of the new CO (alias Gregory Peck). Peck plays the role of a High-D, dominant, no-nonsense leader of men who is highly Task-oriented. Men on their way for some food, sleep or a shower are challenged with the standard military, *'where do you think you are going?'* Clearly, the old regime had passed and the priorities had changed. Now the focus was Task - let's get these planes in the air and get the job done. The inevitable happens, as the missions increase, the care of the men becomes a secondary issue. The Individuals begin to suffer and the Team spirit deteriorates to the point where the Task is endangered. Only a brief synopsis, but the illustration is clear. Which CO was the better leader? Perhaps the cinema-going public would prefer the first CO who cared for the men but John Adair's point was that neither CO was correct. The effective leader is like the plate spinner with three plates - all three have to be spun with equal attention, otherwise the neglected ones will fall and break.

Mutiny on the Bounty contained another example of TTI disharmony. Captain Bligh was an off-the-scale Driver who overstepped the mark of the already very severe disciplinary standards of 1787. His task obsession drove the men to the unthinkable - mutiny, which carried with it the almost certain sentence of hanging. Task was all important and the team began to seethe, but the catalyst was the singling out of an individual or two for exceptionally brutal treatment.

Very dramatic tales, but there are everyday examples. Often a company finds it has some unspent cash in its training budget. Rather than lose it, the manager responsible plans a weekend away for the staff. The typical venue is a country 'spa' hotel with lots of facilities. A couple of consultants are called in to organise some management 'games' and no expense is spared to make the staff feel valued.

Most of these activity weekends do not achieve the desired result. The problems are consistently the same - some members of staff have to travel too far; people were not informed till almost the last minute as to where they were going; some consider the management 'games' silly; most would rather spend their precious weekend at home; the golf course was unplayable because of the weather or the day finished too late to allow the three hours necessary for eighteen holes; the swimming pool was open to local families at weekends and every kid from a ten mile radius was at lung practice; the ten-seater sauna had twelve people in it; the food in The Carvery was lavish but ninety per cent of the staff were on a diet; Mark had to share a room with Gary, and they hate the sight of one another. However these are all symptoms. The disease is that no one really sat down to consider the **Team, Task** and **Individual** implications.

What is the task? To spend the money? Hardly. The **Task** is a team building exercise to motivate, entertain, educate, enthuse, bond and engender loyalty in the staff. The **Team** could be a department or the entire staff and the **Individuals** are those men and women who each have identifiable personalities, wants and needs. The most common mistake is to by-pass the Individuals and simply tell the Team what is planned. Mistake number two is not making it clear what the objective is. This results in people gathering round the office coffee machine saying, *I believe we're going away for the weekend. Where to? What for? Whose idea was this? When are we going? Do we have to go?* And other obvious questions.

Rule one in the TTI success formula is consultation. A staff meeting is essential. Outline the objectives, offer suggestions, give alternatives, seek comment, gain consensus, agree and plan ahead. Even if the event is not particularly brilliant, the fact that the staff were consulted and were part of the decision making process will ensure their support for the plan. Unlike the 'fabulous, exciting paint-balling weekend' thrust upon a reluctant staff, fifty percent of whom were women'. Sure, paint-balling games where people fight in 'jungle warfare' in some damp Hampshire wood can be team building and fun but it is essential that people know all the relevant details. Some may be demotivated by it. Crawling through soggy ferns in battle fatigues and being struck by paint pellets may not make every young female's heart race with excitement. The most basic checks can be overlooked. Some people simply will not share hotel rooms; others think it more fun to have someone convivial to share with.

If a team building exercise ends with mutterings such as, *that was a total waste of time; I'd much rather have been at home ... in the pub ... playing football ... making love,* then the exercise has been a failure.

One extremely successful event was organised by a Scottish company who, having checked out all the prestige 'spa' hotels such as Gleneagles, Dalmahoy, Peebles and Crieff Hydros, contacted a travel agent who organised a three day break in Spain. The mornings were planned for conference work, not in a stuffy room but with a pool-side flip-chart and trays of soft drinks. For the remainder of the day delegates were free to play golf, explore, shop, swim, whatever. Dinner was communal with a brief discussion on the day's conference and agreement was reached on the next day's agenda. Not only was the event a great success but the overall cost to the company was actually marginally cheaper than that for a posh UK venue. Total TTI. The Task was accomplished, the Team was united in their approval and appreciation and the Individual felt valued and had a good time to boot.

The family holiday is another test for TTI. The kids want excitement and fun, Mum would like somewhere sophisticated where staff might wait on her for a change and Dad would like the big outdoors where he could do some fishing. The task is to have a successful family holiday, the team is all the family who should ideally be bonded by the experience and the individual is represented by each one's specific wishes. It is a dilemma chosen as an exemplar not because of its difficulty but because of its recurrence. This is a highly common situation which most families have experienced.

What can happen is that Dad, possibly a Driver or an Inspirer, either insists he gets his way or sells his preferences by inspiring and enthusing his family with a concept they do not really wish for. Alternatively both parents could forego their own preferences and go along with the wishes of the kids. A third option is that a caring father should convince the kids that Mum needed the break most and her wishes were the more important. A fourth if somewhat extreme choice might be - money permitting - that Mum is sent off to the Côte D'Azur, Dad to Stornaway and the kids packed off to Disney Land with some accommodating relative. Perhaps the I factor might be achieved but the two Ts might suffer.

The key to any successful dynamic is to achieve TTI harmony. Often total harmony cannot be achieved, but the further towards extreme disharmony the greater the failure.

A typical situation which we have all seen at some time or another is where the family car is loaded up for a holiday trip. Dad likes to drive. Mum takes a magazine and the kids are provided with every diversion known to mankind. It does not take long before the kids are bored witless with their toys, games and comics. I-spy ran for all of five minutes before they were sick of it. One kid wants Country music, the other wants Rock; Mum, tired of the vacuity of modern magazines, wants The Planets by Holst and Dad wants the news then silence. Then the 'how-much-longer-before-we-get-there' chorus begins. In this situation there is a biological certainty that no two people ever need a lavatory at the same time. It would be a brave management consultant who would offer a solution for this one. The short answer is - don't allow the problem to develop in the first place.

What precisely is the link between the post-war management gurus and personality profiling?

In a phrase - the recognition of personality. Prior to this profound change in management methodology, nobody cared much for personality at all. Workers were treated almost like commodities. What is the maximum calorific output we can extract from these people without literally working them to death? The only reason shifts ran for a finite time was simply to maximise the working potential of the individual. Task-driven, X-style management was the norm. It is prudent to remember that as recently as the 19th century, human beings were imported from Africa, chosen and bred purely for their ability to work.

Abraham Maslow gave us the human being's Hierarchy of Needs. McGregor identified the Theory X and Theory Y styles of management. Adair made it clear that the Team, Task and Individual all had to be balanced.

Yet another guru of the time was Frederick Hertzberg. His book (co-written with B Mausner and B Snyderman), *The Motivation to Work* was very much in tune with Maslow's work. Hertzberg alluded to man's duality of nature in that he had a need as an animal to be comfortable and to avoid pain while at the same time a need to grow psychologically. Maslow would have approved. Hertzberg went on to identify what he called *hygiene factors*. We associate the word with cleanliness but Hertzberg used it in its Greek derivation meaning health. His point was that the worker needed physical and mental health. His list of determining factors included achievement, recognition, the work itself, responsibility, advancement, salary, interpersonal relations and working conditions. He laid out all these hygiene factors on a normative scale and carried out surveys, the better known being with two hundred Pittsburgh engineers and accountants, establishing in a relatively simple marks-out-of-ten type of scoring the contentment factor of each employee.

Interestingly of the ten or more hygiene factors he codified, salary consistently figured in the bottom three.

As each new piece of psychological wisdom was introduced into the world of work there was established a direct correlation between the recognition of personality and productivity.

Taking a random selection of the writings of the post-war industrial psychologists, it now seems striking how similar the titles were,

A Theory of Human Motivation (Maslow)

Need Satisfactions and Employee Turnover (Ross and Zander)

Employee Attitudes and Employee Performance (Brayfield and Crockett)

Job Satisfaction in Relation to Mental Health (Kornhauser)

The Motivation-Hygiene Theory (Hertzberg)

Job Design and Employee Motivation (Lawler)

Social Psychology of the work Organisation (Tannenbaum)

The Motivational Basis of Organisational Behaviour (Katz)

The Human Side of Enterprise (McGregor)

The production of works on occupational psychology was prolific and they spanned roughly a decade from the mid-50s to the mid-60s. Nowadays, we look at these titles and with a superior smile we say, but we know all that, its obvious! Like the laws of gravity or Galileo's earth-shattering discovery that our planet revolved around the sun, we take it for granted that personality is an intrinsic part of the working environment. There is no Eureka factor when we read these titles because not only do we understand how vital the human side of work is but legislation has now ensured that employees have rights and expectations which our forbears could only dream of.

An additional point of note in the breakthrough of post-war industrial psychology is that every writer of any substance was American. There is probably subject matter here for a further book on national attitudes to hierarchical structures. Nor is it an isolated period. Hard on the heels of the Maslow generation came the sales and marketing gurus. Madison Avenue became to marketing what The Louvre is to painting and salesmanship became an almost exclusively US art form producing men such as Dale Carnegie, Frank Bettger, Og

Mandino, Tom Hopkins and Zig Zigler. The trend continues with Tom Peters, Peter Drucker, Anthony Robbins and many others.

The British produced some home-grown gurus such as Sir John Harvey-Jones, Gavin Kennedy, Robin Fielder and the excellent Video-Arts team with John Cleese and other screen personalities. There are some cultural differences to overcome. The US open, in-your-face friendliness, born of an egalitarian classlessness sometimes does not quite gel with the more anally-retentive British. Although the psychology of the big smile and *'Have a nice day'* or *'enjoy your meal'* is understood, it somehow doesn't quite work in the UK. The English hotel receptionist might be carefully schooled to say, *'Good morning, Hotel Bellevue, Tracey speakin' - how may I help you, please.'* But we feel uncomfortable with it. In fairness, it is a bit of a mouthful in any language - also, although the 'please' is well intentioned, semantically it sucks. In Long Beach, it sounds okay but in London it sounds out of kilter with the indigenous speech patterns. The fundamental problem is that the whole ethos of a greeting or any pleasantry is that it is spontaneous, like the smile itself. In any language, a genuinely warm smile and a gracious manner is a delight so when we know that these rather alien expressions are carefully taught, it dampens their very purpose. Similarly, no Brit would think of asking for fish and fries in a standard chip shop but feels obliged to conform with the US vernacular in that shrine to globalisation, McDonald's.

Cultural differences apart, the link between personality and performance is as clear as it is profound. Tom Peters makes the point that a boardroom which is too harmonious is a danger to company health. A High-D CEO surrounded by Yes-men is never going to produce the sparks which are essential to keep a company fired up. To pursue the fire analogy, it takes friction to produce a spark and friction will not be found in a passive boardroom.

A business scenario

The focus of this chapter has been on the formation of teams, types of team, what makes them work and what makes them come asunder.

Stage, screen and family life have been used to illustrate harmony and the clashes of interest. Let us use a business illustration embodying personality and Adair's theme of the TTI dynamic to conclude.

Major corporations often work on a regional basis. Take office equipment manufacturing as an example, companies may be split into a dozen regions. Each region will have a Regional General Manager to whom all departments report. The departments will consist of the Sales Department, the Engineers or Service Department, the Work Control Department and the Administration Department.

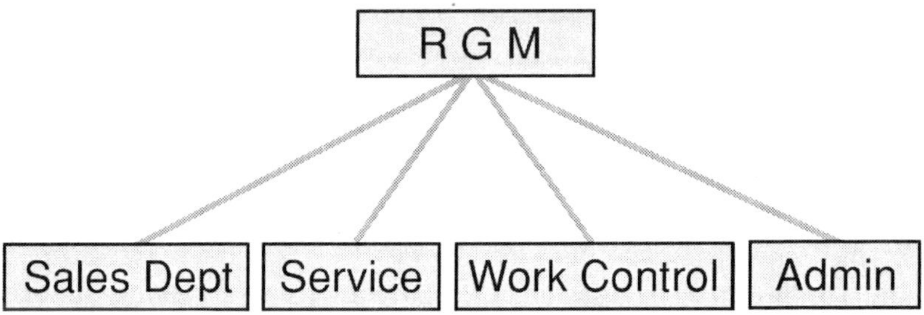

The Sales Department is one team which could be subdivided into smaller teams such as copier sales, computer sales or colour copier sales. The Service Department consists of engineers whose job it is to service and repair all the machines in the field (MIF). This team could also be split into smaller teams depending on their range of skills, i.e. computer repairs, fax repairs etc. Their work is controlled by the Work Control Department who take all incoming service calls, register the requirement and allocate an engineer to the job based on the geographic whereabouts of the nearest engineer. Work Control also monitor in/out job times and maintain departmental performance charts. The Admin team handle everything else including correspondence, invoicing, payment arrears/credit control, secretarial tasks and payroll.

The RGM's job is Plate Spinner in Chief. It is a very difficult task. All teams have to believe they are equal in the pursuit of a common task. All individuals have to feel valued as a member of their departmental team, but also as a member of the wider regional team. Firstly there are the actual differences then the perceived differences.

Sales Department

Often the sales force are seen as being in a rather glamorous role. They wear the smart suits; their cars have to be clean and up to date; the tools of their trade - briefcases, sight-sellers and visual aids have to be slick and professional. Because some salespeople do earn serious amounts of money on some months they can be perceived by others as earning big pay checks every month. When they are top salespeople for a given period, there is usually a presentation at the best local hotel (Maslow in action). At the national conference for all regions, the top salesperson will win some glamorous prize such as a holiday for two in Barbados (on top of the serious money earned). To other departments, this may engender envy which is a first cousin of hate.

The reality of course is quite different. Each month, salespeople have a target to reach. At the monthly meeting, the Regional Sales Manager demands that each team leader makes a commitment on a flip chart of how much revenue the team will bring in. The team leader makes each team member commit to an individual figure, the total of which becomes the leader's commitment. Each team in turn puts its neck on the block. Throughout the month, the figures are monitored weekly or daily. Exhortations or threats are used. With each 'blank' day the pressure on the salesperson grows, so by mid-month if the sales board is still blank, the sales people feel pain. Each rejection can reduce that key quality - confidence.

At the month end, the RSM produces the flip chart commitments and calls each person forward to compare the result with the prediction and explain the difference. Over 100% of target can be exhilarating, well under can be crushing. Next comes the predictions for the forthcoming month and on it goes.

Service Department

Sometimes seen by others as an easy life. Go where you are asked to go. People welcome you when you arrive. Take as long as you need to fix the equipment properly. Clients are delighted to have their machine back in action. Just phone in to Work Control to report the job done and await allocation of the next job. No great initiative needed, no planning required, no rejection whatever. Steady income, no loss of commission if difficulty arises.

Speak to the engineers and the picture is somewhat different. No smart suits or flashy visual aids for them. Often some irate office manager chooses to vent his or her spleen on the repair engineer. More often than not, the problem is caused by misuse of the machine. The engineer may be dismissed as 'just the mechanic' by office girls the same age as his daughter. Engineers complain of 'invisibility' as they crouch on the floor to attack the innards of some mishandled photocopier. No glamour, little respect, no bumper wage packets, no flashy car - more likely a repair van with company logo. The reality of their work can be exacerbated by their perceived notion of a life in Sales.

Work Control

These people have a cushy job. Never have to go out in all weathers facing the unappreciative business world. Always able to take a coffee break; always able to gossip with colleagues; no need for competitive jealousy; as a team always able to cover for one another. Comfortable job, no rejection, never get their hands dirty.

Not quite - these too are front line troops. They take the calls, the abuse, the follow-up calls if an engineer is late; they take lip back from the engineers for allocating a job too far away or too protracted for the time of day. They never get outside the office to get some fresh air; if they are smokers, they have to stand in an alley for their nicotine fix - you get the picture. Admin is a similar story.

Here we have the perception of the role and the reality of it. The RGM's job is to monitor, value, praise, fault, guide and encourage all the departments as equals. When the TTI balance is at its best, the results can be impressive. Sometimes the RGM may be of an Admin background so he will focus more on that department. He may not fully understand the frustrations and depressions of the sales or service departments. He may even make derogatory remarks about smart-arsed sales people.

More often he or she is from a sales background and, even unwittingly, lays more emphasis on the sales effort than on the other teams.

A neutral observer will deduce quickly that if any one department fails in its departmental task, the entire dynamic will go out of kilter and the business would collapse. The sales people will argue that if they don't sell the boxes, nobody works. Service people resent this saying the products are only as good as the service they receive. Work control and Admin have equally valid claims on the success of the dynamic.

If the RGM is an Inspirer, he may lack empathy with the Admin Department. As a Co-ordinator he may lack the gift to drive the sales force. Juggle as you may with the TTI dynamic and the DISC permutations of the RGM but the bottom line is always personality.

More people leave jobs because of personality clashes, stress, cliques, favouritism, discrimination and an overall unpleasant atmosphere than because of workload or pay and conditions.

Footnote

In two similar corporations to the above, I introduced the simple practice of the engineers spending a day with a salesperson and vice versa until all individuals had spent at least one day in every team. Once accomplished, I then asked all staff if they wished to apply for a team change. No takers. Relieved of their misconceptions, they accepted the reality of the status quo; more importantly individuals developed a greater respect for one another and the result was a more positive TTI dynamic.

I also introduced a 'generic' Appraisal Form which could be applied by almost any manager in almost any working environment. The idea for the form was taken entirely from John Adair's principle of the TTI dynamic. Several companies I have worked with as a consultant chose to use the Appraisal Form as a basis for their own company personnel practices. The Form consists of questions from the perspective of the three elements.

TASK RELATED QUESTIONS

General conscientiousness	1	2	3	4
Willingness to take on tasks	1	2	3	4
Structured approach to tasks	1	2	3	4
Evidence of organisational planning	1	2	3	4
Evidence of Time Management	1	2	3	4
Willingness to seek help	1	2	3	4
Willingness to accept help	1	2	3	4
Evidence of Initiative towards tasks	1	2	3	4
Eagerness to get the job done	1	2	3	4
Makes suggestions to help overall task	1	2	3	4
General record of achievement	1	2	3	4
Attention to detail	1	2	3	4

TEAM RELATED QUESTIONS

Friendliness towards colleagues	1	2	3	4
Helpfulness towards colleagues	1	2	3	4
Willingness to stand-in for colleagues	1	2	3	4
Takes thorough and clear messages for others	1	2	3	4
Ensures messages reach colleagues	1	2	3	4
Sees overall objective of team's task	1	2	3	4
Considerate of other's needs	1	2	3	4

INDIVIDUAL RELATED QUESTIONS

Punctuality - work, appointments, meetings	1	2	3	4

Manner - on phone, to customers, colleagues	1	2	3	4
Appearance - dress, grooming, deportment	1	2	3	4
Cheerful and companionability	1	2	3	4
Reaction to authority	1	2	3	4
Dependability	1	2	3	4
Ability to say No to minor distractions	1	2	3	4
Evidence of ambition	1	2	3	4
Evidence of managerial ability	1	2	3	4
Earns respect of colleagues	1	2	3	4
Earns trust of colleagues	1	2	3	4
Evidence of self motivation	1	2	3	4
Enthusiasm	1	2	3	4
Confidence	1	2	3	4
Persistence / Perseverance	1	2	3	4

Clearly any company can add or adjust the questions listed to suit its own modus operandi, but The principle remains - there are only three strands to making an organisation work and if an employee is performing well in all three fields, then we are on the way to success.

In the light of 4QB one has to be careful when awarding a point to areas such as Enthusiasm or confidence. One has to allow for the Introvert-Extrovert scale.

Recommended marking:

1 : Unacceptable 2 : Acceptable 3 : Good 4 : Exemplary

Avoid an odd number of columns for rating as weaker managers may just opt for the middle figure.

Naturally, the form will need all the other standard ingredients of an appraisal form such as:

Recommendations for improvement

Training undergone
Training required
Manager's comments
Employee's comments
... and so on

6

The Human Side

Although every aspect of personality relates to humanity, the emphasis so far has been mainly concerning the working environment, management applications or stage and screen representation. One regular question at lectures on personality profiling is which quadrants are likely to form good loving relationships. Blaise Pascal put it better than most in the 17th century when he said *'The Heart has its Reasons which Reason knows Nothing of'*. All management applications are based on an intelligent appraisal of personality type. Love has little to do with the intellect. Moreover, a popular fictional theme is the match of the 'unsuitable' such as Romeo and Juliet, The Prince and the Showgirl or that torch bearer, Beauty and the Beast. The Arab Omar Sharif even caused offence in the Middle East by his on-screen kiss with the Jewish Barbara Streisand in Funny Girl.

'Make Me a Match, Catch Me a Catch'

Perhaps the nearest working application in finding the most suitable match for the unattached is to be found in the Lonely Heart Bureaux. Some of these professional matchmakers will require quite lengthy questionnaires to be completed so that, when recommending a meeting, they will avoid the more obvious pitfalls. Clearly it might not be prudent to send Yasser Arafat's nephew out on a date with Ariel Sharon's niece. Although the matchmakers will not consciously use psychometric tests they will deduce from the hobbies, interests and occupations a certain personality profile which they would try to blend with a near match. A home loving guy who is a great TV fan whose greatest pleasure is pizza and beer in front of his favourite programme might not make a gal's heart race if she just adores mountain walks, swimming and camping. But they are only common sense guidelines. When the athletic Joe Di Maggio married the body beautiful Marilyn Monroe, it seemed a good match but not long after they split she married the intellectual Arthur Miller. *Vous avez raison*, M. Pascal.

Because of the subject's very unquantifiable and indefinable nature, little research has been carried out. One closer look was taken by Charles Handy in his book *The Age of Unreason*. Handy also uses the four base types of D, I, S and C - only he calls them by different names. In the table shown on page xx in Chapter two, the top line shows Choleric, Sanguine, Phlegmatic and Melancholic while the bottom line shows the terms Handy chose - Thruster, Involved, Caring and Loners. These names correspond with DISC. What does a Thruster sound like - pushy, assertive, dominant, yes very much the Driver. Involved? Sound very much like an Inspirer, always involved in company, chatting, wanting to know what's going on etc. Caring? No comment needed. And the Loner? Again sounds very much like someone who is thoughtful, self-contained, reflective and analytical - our C.

In the research he carried out, Handy found that there was no overwhelming preponderance of any two quadrants being drawn to each other in any statistically significant way. However there were sufficiently consistent recurrences to make his research valid. He found the top four matches were:

1. Thrusting male with a Caring female
2. two Involveds
3. two Loners
4. two Thrusters.

The No 1 spot comes as no great surprise. It is by far the most common matching used in fiction and drama. Certainly in all Western movies it became a cliché. The rugged hero riding across the plain leaving a trail of dust; the passive, sweet-natured wife spots him in the distance as she winds the bucket up from the well. She dashes into the cabin to 'purty herself up' and adjust her gingham dress. As he clasps her to his manly chest she all but swoons and the audience gives a satisfied 'Ahh'. It just would not work with two High Ds. Imagine John Wayne sliding off his saddle to be greeted by an irate High-D such as Margaret Thatcher.

'Get you some whiskey! Get your own bloody whiskey, and look at the state of those trousers, what on earth have you been doing in them? No, don't you come near me till you've had a damn good bath, you smell of sweat and cow shit. And another thing - you said you'd be back in April, it's now June, where the hell have you been? Food, food is it. There's some bread on the table, I'm off to the Dodge City Townswomen's Assertiveness Class.'

The D Robin Hood and the S Maid Marion, Heathcliffe and Cathy, the tough gangster and the devoted moll - always an on-screen favourite. This is not to say that other quadrant mixes don't make good cinema, not at all, just watch Elizabeth Taylor and Richard Burton in *Who's Afraid of Virginia Woolf* - two High Ds who fought like cat and dog yet somehow were drawn inexorably together. Or Gene Kelly and Debbie Reynolds as two Inspirers in *Singin' in The Rain* - magic. No, the point is that historically the most popular male/female pairing with fictional characters has been D/S so it is not unreasonable to extrapolate from this that human nature will more commonly aspire to this blend.

However, to be ruthlessly realistic, there are inherent dangers in the D/S mix. We are all conscious of the attraction of opposites so a Supporting woman might find a Dominant male very attractive and reassuring to have around. Conversely he might find a passive, caring woman provides that softer side of personality which he lacks. Initially this may prove very satisfactory to both but the risk is that over time those very differences may be a cause of irritation and rancour. How often have we heard the more passive wife say to an assertive husband,

'You're always so damned sure of yourself. You've always got to be

right haven't you. It never occurs to you that I or others might have an opinion. You're so intolerant ...'

It often takes time. In the beginning, the Supporter quite likes decisiveness and firmness, also a pattern becomes established. He asserts, she concurs and on it goes until it goes against the grain to contradict, but pressure can build up to the point where the Supporter may need to let off some pent-up steam. This can come as a surprise to the Driver male who has become inured to the pattern and, as sensitivity is not a strong suit with the Driver, he may not have noticed the signals that a head of steam was building up. We should never underestimate the Supporters; just because their preference is to care and perhaps soothe does not mean they lack the capacity to be strong and say, thus far and no further. There have been many dramatic examples such as in the Thatcher Government, one Cabinet Minister, Geoffrey Howe felt he had taken enough of being overruled and dismissed by his Driver Prime Minister. Geoffrey had once been ridiculed by Labour's Denis Healy when Healy had described being attacked by Howe as 'like being savaged by a dead sheep'. In truth, Howe always did appear remarkably passive and undemonstrative so it was all the more sensational when Howe, in a prepared speech in the House, denounced Mrs Thatcher with some quite extraordinarily strong criticisms.

Supporters tend to be loyal and principled but our first loyalty is always to ourselves. An interesting development in jurisprudence in the last couple of decades is the number of S wives who have murdered brutal D husbands yet have walked free from the courts. We have come a long way from the last hanging of a woman in Britain, some fifty years ago. Ruth Ellis had been cheated on by her playboy lover. Her distress was so profound that she shot him dead. She was found guilty of murder and was hanged.

What always surprises people is when the Supporter wife can take no more and kills her husband. They always comment, *she seemed so quiet, wouldn't say boo to a goose, never thought she'd be capable of such an act ...* The corollary of such comments is that the action is more consistent with a fiery, Driver temperament. Perhaps it is, but in a Driver/Driver relationship or Thruster/Thruster in Charles Handy's terminolgy, the male would never get so far in the mistreatment of his wife. One offensive or violent action by him and she would make it crystal clear that she would not stand for such behaviour. Moreover such males are often bullies and bullies more often than not lack courage, so one unequivocal warning from the woman could be enough to rein in his behaviour. Who can forget the Bobbit case in the US where Mr Bobbit had been seriously unfaithful to his woman. Taking a sharp implement while Mr Bobbit slept, she removed the offending organ with one unerring cut. Whether Mr Bobbit was reattached to the missing organ one cannot remember but one thing is absolutely certain, the likelihood of Mr Bobbit re-offending is minimal (whether through lacking the wherewithal so to do or out of profound fear of the consequences, matters not). Such a highly decisive - not to mention painful - action is wholly consistent with a not-to-be-messed-with High-D.

The physical equivalent of the verbal outburst where the wife rebels with, *you're always so damn right, aren't you* is where the dominance degenerates to physical repression of the wife. Some of the cases before the courts are so dreadful as to defy belief; wives who have undergone physical cruelty for literally years. Defence counsels have produced case histories of punches, broken bones, facial disfigurement and a whole range of appalling batterings. Our reaction is one of disgust and disbelief varying in incomprehension depending on our own personality quadrant.

For balance we should also examine the flip side of the D/S interaction. While the S may find the perpetual assertion of the D wearing and tiresome over time, leading to the type of outburst shown, the D may find dissatisfaction also. What initially attracted him was her sweetness of nature, her non-confrontational style and her easy acquiescence. In time, this may irritate him leading to outbursts such as:

Don't be so damned soft. Go right back to that store and complain like hell. What do you mean you don't want to make a fuss, you've every damn right to make a fuss. Don't give in to the kids so easily, you'll spoil them. Just tell them no.

And so on. While opposites do attract, they are still opposites. In a solid, loving relationship these opposites should not detract from the match but if the fire of lurve should dwindle or even go out, the opposites could exacerbate any divide rather than help unite.

IQ

One facet of a human being which a personality profile will not reveal is intelligence. We need other psychometric tests, such as an IQ test or one of Raven's Progressive Matrices to establish this.

It is said that violence is the product of an exhausted mind. All the more so when a mind is easily exhausted. A Driver with a high IQ is not a problem. His preference is to assert, to drive, to dominate and if he has the gift of lucid thought, well constructed argument and articulate delivery, all his assertion can flow out in verbal exchange. In a court of law, a highly intelligent lawyer who is a Driver can be an impressive act to witness. However if the IQ is low, the wish to assert is still foremost but, lacking the necessary articulacy, the Driver may display aggression, partially motivated by internal frustration. We've all witnessed this in some form or another, perhaps in a complaint scenario in a store or a restaurant or some altercation in a motoring situation. How often have we heard the appeal, calm down, keep your hair on, don't lose your head and others. The lack of articulate delivery leads to upping the volume, shouting, then swearing which is often a form of replacement for the words which the angry D cannot find. The next step in this ascending scale (or perhaps descending in a sociological sense) of assertion is violence.

The High-I with a low IQ is seldom a problem. His preference is to inspire to mix, to party. He is the one for whom canned laughter was designed. You can see him in the bar watching TV and commenting, *this is funny*. It may not actually be funny but the accompanying laughter sets the mood. And anyway, who cares - if the guy is enjoying himself and laughs on cue with the soundtrack, good luck to him. However, back to relationships and that emotive subject - Lurve.

The above is only a cautionary word on the inherent dangers in a

D/S match. The intention is not to pour any cold water on that particular match. Most of them are happy, successful relationships. Some even defy any conventional rules. The British Member of Parliament Alan Clark displayed all the qualities of a Driver. That, along with his privileged, upper class background and his rugged good looks gave him the self assurance of a grandee of another era. He had a string of extra-marital affairs, many of which were covered in detail in the press. His wife was the epitome of all that is sweet, passive and resigned - a 100% Supporter. When asked for comment from the press she simply shrugged her shoulders with a, 'that's Alan for you' smile. Quite extraordinary by conventional standards, though the greatest mystery of all has to be another politician, Jeffrey Archer. His saga of deceit, disloyalty, dishonesty and a few other dis-s takes some beating even in the annals of that chamber of the dim and dissolute, the House of Lords, yet his profoundly intelligent and self-sufficient wife stands resolutely by him. In a test paper, the preceding sentence would by followed by, 'Discuss'.

Perhaps the very power of the D/S magnetism is such as to continue to make it the No 1 match but this is doubtful. The nurture factor might in the past have bred females who admired a dominant male just as young men considered the strong silent type to be a role model. The volume of sexist phraseology was once overwhelming, most of it patronising and dismissive towards women. Now with women, the norm in what once were considered male professions including all branches of the armed forces, the days of the imagery of the masterful male and the submissive female are numbered.

While Cupid can strike us from any angle, same quadrant relationships make a great deal of sense. The attraction of opposites will always wield a power but as in a D/S relationship, there are inherent risks in all opposites. The High-C may find the High-I entertaining and stimulating. While the C likes to internalise and savour experiences, the I needs to externalise, explore, discuss and respond. The Coordinator can feel that the Inspirer is filling a dimension which the C lacks and in company or at parties it can be a comfort to watch the I effortlessly mix and be agreeable to all. The risk, quite naturally, is that the Inspirer may become tiresome, always speculating, examining, moving from idea to idea or person to person. To the more reflective C, the very difference can become an area of extreme irritation. Conversely the Inspirer might have found the C a bit of a challenge because Inspirers love to draw people out, evoke a response or a laugh. The very deepness, calmness and introvertedness may appear very interesting to the Inspirer. Again, over time, the sniping comments are not uncommon.

'When we get there, don't make me do all the talking. Introduce yourself to people, don't expect me to do it all the time - and circulate, don't be at my elbow all night - and don't correct my stories'

Charles Handy's No 2, 3 and 4 spots are all 'same quadrant' matches. With the demise of Dominant/Submissive imagery, it would be interesting to carry out Handy's survey again in the 21st Century. Same quadrant matches have a lot going for them - take two Coordinators. Others might snigger while two Cs pore over their collection of rare early 20th Century stamps or the fossils they have collected from a geologically significant beach or perhaps at their specialist holiday where their time is spent on an archaeological dig. They might simply enjoy the peaceful communion of silently reading their chosen books. Who knows, not perhaps the stuff movies are made of but such deep compatibility has a great deal more going for it as a long term relationship than matches from opposite quadrants.

Similarly with two Inspirers who both love to talk, to explore, to laugh and to see the bright side of things. These two optimists should get along fine. One thing they'll have to watch for is paying bills, managing household accounts, planning and the hundred and one domestic details required in running a home.

Two Caring Supporters would generate a very sweet natured atmosphere at home. Neither would offend the other or hurt the other's feelings. Neither would be late without phoning the other in advance. In fact, the more one dwells on such a household, the more ideal it seems. It might not make a good movie; you can hear the audience leaving the theatre, '*Saccharin nonsense, gooey, lovey-dovey gush, didn't you just want to shake the pair of them*'.

The theory is sound but no doubt the world will continue to make its decisions on an endless set of complex values. Women will continue to spurn the ultra decent boy next door and go for the bad guy with the bad reputation from the other side of the tracks. Intellectually, she probably knows that it is not a wise move but her hormones have already made the decision for her. On the dotted line below insert your own cliché

....

Charisma

Like the man who could not describe an African elephant but knew one when he saw one, it's the same with Charisma, you can't quite put your finger on what it is but you know it when you see it. Better trace its root first.

Don't suppose this comes from the Greek as well? You guessed it! Charis is the Greek for grace, and charisma is said to be a grace or spiritual power given by God. A more earthy description is that which enables someone to impress or influence others.

Is there a 4QB predominance here?

You would think there might be. Words like impress and influence would have the compass twitching towards the Inspirer quadrant but there seems to be an even-handedness in the distribution of charisma. Certainly, High-Is like Bill Clinton had charisma. Even people who have attended his speeches determined not to be impressed, came away with a feeling of inspiration. Jack Kennedy had charisma but he came from further north, more of a Driver, probably an Inspiring Driver. His inaugural speech in January '61 with the line *'ask not what your country can do for you; ask what you can do for your country'* struck a chord of inspiration in most American hearts. To be blunt, the statement is a somewhat vacuous piece of hyperbole. It does not survive a High-C style analysis or close scrutiny from any quadrant for that matter, but it sounded like a line from The Sermon on the Mount. In the battle for hearts and minds, it is significant that hearts get first mention and this exhortation was not aimed at American minds, it was aimed at big, generous, patriotic American hearts. It was a bullseye - but it took the Kennedy charisma to deliver it.

Clinton too had the gift. In Northern Ireland, perhaps one of the most hard-nosed and cynical parts of the globe, Clinton's speeches evoked the name of God and a world of peace akin to Martin Luther King's memorable and moving *I Have a Dream* address. People can smell a phoney or insincerity a mile away yet the citizens of Northern Ireland responded with a wave of warmth to Clinton. Whatever it is, he had it.

Martin Luther King had enormous charisma yet his quadrant was different again, more a Supporting Inspirer. Tiny, fragile and painfully thin, Mother Theresa had charisma. Never the best orator nor the most eloquent, yet one public address and world leaders lent an ear; Sweden awarded her the Nobel Peace Prize and Queen Elizabeth gave her the highest British award, the Order of Merit. Her quadrant? S/C? Possibly or maybe a C with 'wings' of S and D. Many a quiet reflective ascetic - High-C - has been charismatic. So, though charismatics influence us, they can be extrovert or introvert, thinkers or feelers. Nor is IQ greatly significant, Prince Charles had a lightly patronising attitude towards Diana's absence of academic achievement, yet it was she who had the charisma.

Dr David Weeks, a consultant clinical neuropsychologist at Royal Edinburgh Hospital explained, *'it could be some way of behaving to people. It could be a person's appearance or how they behave in a one-to-one situation. It is also how much attention they show to people in a very positive way. It could be because they look very good or they have a strong ethic. It could be having a good rapport or getting across a sense of sincerity.*' Reassuring that the good Doctor doesn't know either.

His point about sincerity and being positive strikes a chord. For example, although Prince Charles could talk to people at length, his questions were often a model of good manners and courteous interest, whereas when Diana went amongst the AIDS victims, she did exude sincerity and heartfelt concern. Bill Clinton's rather emotional words to the people of Northern Ireland could have sounded saccharin or phoney from someone else but he did convey that degree of sincerity which wins people over.

The qualities common to the charismatic are self-assurance and a mix of conviction and confidence. Sean Connery has no pretensions to be an intellectual yet his presence both on and off screen has a self-assurance without a trace of braggadocio which makes him one of the most charismatic stars ever. He is also a man of great conviction as any studio or movie producer has found should they have attempted to short-change him. When many men would be content to live a life of luxury, Connery is a stalwart supporter of a political cause, Scottish Independence.

Whether for good or evil, charisma is equally distributed. Hitler had extraordinary charisma in a very assertive form. Osama bin Laden also, but of a more detached and subdued and reflective form. Charisma can be a force for great good as witnessed in the large numbers of women who chose to abandon all worldly comforts and follow Mother Theresa to devote themselves to the poor, the sick and the dying. The converse is also depressingly true, charisma can be a force for evil, as in the numbers of so-called religious leaders who have developed fanatical followings to the point where they will commit mass suicide.

The job interview

The focus of this chapter is on the day-to-day human aspect of personalities so the job interview might seem to belong in the realms of business applications. Perhaps it does for the professional Personnel Manager but, for the vast majority of human beings, it is an experience which all of us have undergone, often many times. The Personnel Manager has a whole kit of professional tools to use - numeracy and literacy tests, IQ tests, personality profiles, application forms, interview skills, role plays, assessment centres and more. For the rest of us, all we have is a CV and a tongue in our heads. Many people who read books about psychometric tests do so because they are concerned about the dreaded job interview. People often ask, just what is the interviewer looking for? How do I know if my profile matches theirs? What questions should I ask? What questions am I likely to be asked? along with a wide range of other questions including what tests they might expect to be given and the best way to respond to them.

It is impossible to gauge precisely what is in the mind of the interviewer. How many of us have thought that a particular job specification was so fitting that it seemed it had been written specifically for us, yet after producing a beautifully prepared letter and adjusting the CV so all the emphases are in the right places, we find we are not even given an interview or worse, the increasingly common and ignorant practice of not replying at all. We shake our heads and say, that job was made for me.

Let us try to ease the pain a little. After years in the world of recruitment and training, let me address this human minefield from both sides of the interview desk.

Our perception is our reality

We perceive the job offered to be perfect for us because we see the vacancy in a certain light. Our imagery entirely conditions our approach to the interview. Two people witnessing the same fracas in a bar or road accident or maybe a daylight robbery, will often give the police wholly different accounts of what happened. Height variations, descriptions of clothing, colour of clothing, makes of car and the hundred and one items of detail the police need are often so dissimilar as to render testimony totally confusing. That is from people who have witnessed the same event, so when an employer has a firm perspective of the vacancy he wishes to fill and we have a firm perspective of how suitable we are, as often as not the two pictures do not match.

My face didn't fit

Often we say it in a rather accusatory tone. In fact we could be dead right. The employer may have a predetermined piece of visual imagery or a prejudice fixed in his or her head. The most obvious being sexism or racial prejudice. I remember only too well recruiting for some Executive position when my PA whispered almost theatrically, *'the next one's a woman!'* Granted nine tenths of the applicants had been men which statistically had to be reflected in the interview ratios but clearly a prejudice existed. Racial prejudice still exists. Among the several thousand delegates who have attended my training courses and lectures, the percentage of black faces was dramatically disproportionate to the ethnic mix of society as a whole.

But faces not fitting can be caused by many forms of prejudice. The selector may have some hazy image of the type of person required to fit the bill. This is unfair and unprofessional but life ain't fair. Survey after survey has shown that good-looking people will stand a better chance than ugly people, slim applicants have a head start on fat ones. You put on your smartest suit, your shoes are gleaming and everything about you is sparklingly professional, but the interviewer is a where-there's-muck-there's-brass Yorkshireman or one of those from the I-came-up-the-hard-way school. Your accent is too down-market or too up-market. The frustration is that we never know for sure what it is that triggered the rejection. One experiment carried out in the UK was where a range of applications were sent for a number of disparate vacancies. Half the letters used names such as John Brown, the other half were signed using surnames such as Hussein, Patel and Singh. You guessed it, the invitation to interview was disproportionately much higher for Group A.

One panel interview I was involved in was where a staff member, Chris, recommended a friend, Joe, for a training position. Quite a common occurrence and some companies pay a 'bounty' to the person making the recommendation if the application is successful. The applicant was asked to make a presentation to a group of trainers plus a couple from the Personnel Department. The content of the presentation was okay but the style was extremely flat and lifeless. The applicant left the room while we discussed the presentation and awarded marks for 'the big three' - Content, Style and Delivery. Joe's Content was good but even after allowing for nervousness and tension, all of the battle-hardened trainers considered that Joe's Style and Delivery would die when faced with twenty feisty salespeople. The next stage was to invite Joe back to face a panel interview. In the meantime Chris excused himself and left the room.

When Joe came back for the interview, we all noticed a distinct delivery change. Joe answered every question with little jokes, a nervous laugh and a determined attempt to be buoyant. The penny didn't take long to drop - Chris had spoken with Joe and said he'd need to lighten up a bit. Poor Joe did his best, but the conflict between natural self and this sudden new persona was so apparent as to spoil the interview even further.

All this - before we even get to the 4QB balance between interviewer and interviewee. It can be an infuriating process. We'll come to 4QB interaction in a minute but let us get some basics right first. Every personnel or management magazine focuses on the following points with great regularity. No recruitment section of a newspaper is without the dos and don'ts of job applications for very long.

At the risk of insulting the reader's intelligence, it might be worth devoting a few words to them. It's okay - this is for grown-ups, there'll be no mention of polished shoes and combing one's hair.

- Read the advertisement.
- Adapt your CV to the ad.
- Discard the irrelevant.
- Prepare your questions.
- Write down your questions (two copies).
- Research the company (SWOT).
- Use open questions.
- Do not focus on pay and conditions.
- Don't ask about the company car (where relevant).
- Remember Content - Style - Delivery.

Read the Ad.

Not as obvious as it seems. Read the ad aloud. Take a highlighter pen and mark the key words in the advertisement. Don't be put off if it says 'preferably a graduate' or specifies some element of experience or qualification that you do not have. As in all negotiations, people have three levels of what they want:

Like to get - Expect to get - Must get

Some employers actually make quite stupid demands. How often have you seen something like, *'a graduate with at least three years experience in management, a proven track record of successful business development'* then an idiotic *'aged 25 to 30'*. The age specification is now illegal in many countries but it still occurs in the UK. The advertiser is after the impossible. He wants someone who is brilliant, young, dynamic, experienced, successful, of managerial calibre - Mr or Ms Perfect. Mission impossible. Firstly, if a graduate, the person will have left college around age 21 or 22. The likelihood of someone having several years management experience and a good track record of business development and be around 25 years of age is nonsense. Even at 30, the odds are quite long. Also, would someone so successful in a managerial position be firing off CVs to companies who have not really thought through their specifications. This is what the employer would *Like to get*. The employer's *expect to get* bracket will be more realistic and he may well settle for his *must get*. Also would you really want someone who went straight from college to some hard nosed business and worked like hell to be a success. Much better someone who's taken some time out, seen a bit of the world, made some mistakes and learned a little about life.

Alas, the *like to get* is all too frequent. Companies advertise for plate-spinners. 'Hard working, self-starters, proven track-record, able to work on own initiative, ready to travel, work long hours, good team player, work hard, play hard, determined, a burning desire to succeed'. Made up comments? No - all lifted directly from the recruitment pages of the daily press.

Adapt your CV to the ad.

You'll hear people tell you that they chose a dozen or so ads from the press and sent the same CV off to every one. They will bemoan the absence of replies. Far better to send fewer CVs but adjust each one to the ad you have read so carefully. Draw attention to the appropriate paragraph in your letter, i.e. *'You'll see that from July 2000 to January 2002 I was closely involved in …'* Or *'I have highlighted those areas which I consider are directly relevant to your vacancy'*. When being interviewed, you will often notice that this is precisely what the interviewer has done. You may not be able to read the text upside down but frequently you will notice that certain of your details have been underscored or picked out in yellow.

Your accompanying letter should use as many of the terms used in the advertised vacancy. *'You seek someone with sound experience in advertising sales. For three years I ...'* If a university degree is specified and you don't have one yet you feel you could do the job, say why. No need to say you don't have the qualification. No point telling lies though, as this will inevitably cause pain later on.

Discard the irrelevant

You don't have to delete the irrelevant from the CV but diminish the description to a few lines, e.g. *'97 - 99, two years out in Australia; bar work, taxi driver, swimming instructor and door to door sales.'*

Prepare your questions

It really impresses and pleases prospective employers when they ask if you have any questions and you reply, *'Eleven, to be precise'*. These are very easy to prepare using Kipling's Six. You are probably familiar with Rudyard Kipling's little ditty;

I had six serving men
They taught me all I knew
Their names were What and Why and When
And Where and How and Who.

Straight away you could formulate fifty questions if you wished just using Kipling's Six. Who started the company? When? What was the turnover then? What is it now? How many employees? Where did the company begin? Where are the company's branches? When did you join the company? In What capacity? Where had you been before? Clearly you don't want to overdo it. Your reply, 'Yes I've got eighty-seven questions' might not be greeted with the same level of enthusiasm.

Write down your questions (2 copies)

This really looks good. *Yes, I have, let me see, eight questions, which I have here - I'll just pass you a copy.* Cool.

Research the company

While intelligent questions show an excellent approach to the company, do try to acquire an overview of the company before you attend the interview. A man who sold the services of a management consultancy always, before he made his appointed sales call, received from his head office a profile of the target company. Three years management accounts, names of directors, company history and more. When he then spoke with the appropriate board member(s) his knowledge seemed encyclopaedic and most impressive.

Marketing people call this a SWOT Analysis. Stands for Strengths, Weaknesses, Opportunities, Threats. These four areas would include an understanding of the market place, any USPs (unique selling points) of the product, the competition and the way the market place is growing/contracting.

Not that anyone is suggesting a job applicant should go to such lengths, but you'll grasp the principle.

Use open questions

All Kipling's Six are 'open' questions and elicit much more information than closed questions, i.e. *Are the hours 9 - 5?* Yes. *Do you have a canteen?* No. *Is there a company car?* Yes. Hard work.

Don't focus on pay and conditions (or company car)

Naturally, you will want to know a few basics, but don't focus on them. Ask any (e.g.) sales manager his pet hate questions and the answer will be, *What make of car do you provide. Is that the 1600cc or the 1800cc. LX or GLX model. What's the annual holiday entitlement. How does the holiday year run.* While these questions are quite natural, the mind-set they convey is very much the what's-in-it-for-me one. There is an abundance of time to sort out these details. By being coolly aloof from such non-essential detail (to the employer anyway) and focusing on the job, its requirements and the company's expectations, the image conveyed is of greater professionalism. Also there is usually a second interview, an offer of employment then a contract of employment. The minor details (they may not be minor to you) can all be tacked down later.

Remember : Content, Style, Delivery

When teaching Presentation Skills, the three strands of the course were Content, Style and Delivery. A job interview has much in common with a presentation. First decide on the content. What you are going to say about yourself. What achievements you are proud of. Your relevant experiences. Consider the likely probing questions which might be put to you, such as *'why did you leave that job'* - *'you weren't with that company very long'* - *'you say you were frustrated and could do better; explain that'*. This type of questioning is not of the 'trick questions' genre but simply a desire to understand. One method of interview preparation is to ask a friend to read your CV and play devil's advocate, firing as many challenging questions at you as possible. You'll find the content of what you say becomes very sharp indeed, shorn of any uncertainties and waffle. After Content comes Style and Delivery but we'll leave the latter two for inclusion under the 4QB interview mix.

The Dominant as Interviewer

Not difficult to spot. From the greeting, the High-D personality type manifests itself.

Not too many courtesies, maybe none at all. No preliminary chat such as *'did you find the place all right?'* or *'how was your journey?'* More like *'Susan Smith? - Okay come in take a seat'*. Brief, curt, to the point. The offer of coffee or other refreshment is unlikely. Not rudeness, just very low priority to a High-D. A Driver may place goalposts such as, *'right, Susan; this is a preliminary interview and should take about half an hour. I want to ask you some questions about yourself and your experience, then you ask me anything you want. That okay with you? Right, firstly...'* A High-D might not bother with goalposts and just kick straight off, *'Okay Susan, explain how you see the job and tell me why you think you can do it.'*

With Drivers, generalisations should be avoided as should indeterminate comment, like *'well, I think I might be quite good at this work'* or *'that sounds pretty well the type of thing I might like to do'*. Drivers are too direct for any vagueness and their responses are likely to be, *'what do you mean you think you might be quite good at it?'* or *'what do you mean it sounds pretty well the type of thing you might like?'*

We've covered the 4QB types too well to need dwell on their behaviour as interviewers. In essence, say what you can do and why. Rehearse bullet points in readiness. 'Why do you think you can do this job?' - 'Five reasons!' That is the language the Driver likes. So it may not be a Driver - fine, keep the content, just adapt the delivery or style. Drivers use a lot of direct and forceful questions - their preference is not to tiptoe around an issue - so don't be afraid to respond in kind, with, for example:

- *How many people are you interviewing?*
- *How many have you seen so far?*
- *What made you select my CV?*
- *What start date have you in mind?*
- *When will you get back to me?*

Two benefits in your firing off some direct questions, first - Drivers appreciate that type of approach; second - you will get direct non-evasive answers.

Other aspects of the D type. They will probably take very few notes. The interview will be very straight and entirely verbal. Producing pages of references, documents and certificates will not make much of a difference to the Driver. Drivers are not from Jung's Sensing hemisphere but belong in his Intuitive hemisphere. They'll decide if they like you and if you can cut the mustard quite quickly. Most testimonials and references will go unread by the D.

The Inspirer as Interviewer

Like the Driver, quite easy to identify. One of Jung's Extroverts and also an Intuitive. You'll see it in the greeting - open, looks you straight in the eye, cheery, big on handshaking, a few pleasantries, a joke perhaps. Hospitable - probably offer a coffee? (Accept it). Big gestures; use of arms and hands. Problem with Inspirers is that they will tend to tell you about the company. A High-I may go on at some length, origin of company, development of it, their personal place in the company, their achievements and responsibilities. You, the interviewee, have this wonderful story to tell; you have polished up your **Content**, you've chosen an easy yet positive **Delivery** and your **Style** - having identified the Inspirer - is going to be friendly, enthusiastic, optimistic, big picture oriented and full of 'can do' terminology. Trouble is you can't get a word in edgeways. Eventually the Inspirer will say, 'well, that's enough about us, now tell me a bit about yourself'. You think you have a clear run but it wont be long before the Inspirer interrupts you with a personal anecdote or some other distraction. Here the importance of preparing your Content or Bullet Points which you must get across, is manifest.

What impresses Inspirers is a 'Can Do' attitude. Lots of positive feedback - *'Yes I'd enjoy the challenge'*, *'Irregular hours - doesn't' bother me, I've never been a 9 to 5 clock watcher'*. That sort of thing.

But Inspirers do wander, they can hop from point to point so do have a clear list of the points you feel you must make. Nothing is more irritating than standing outside the interviewer's office clicking your fingers saying, *'Damn, I forget to tell him that ... and I meant to tell him about ...'* Another problem with the Inspirer is that you may hear, *'Thanks very much for coming in Chris, enjoyed talking with you. Leave it with me and I'll get back to you in a few days'*. The High-I probably means it but the nature of the beast is that, like a butterfly, their minds can flit from idea to idea or person to person and 'a few days' can become a week, two weeks or a month. Chase-up phone calls will get you a big friendly *'Oh Hi Chris, not forgotten you, hasn't Susan written to you yet. Okay leave it with me, I'll sort it out'*.

The Supporter as Interviewer

This is very common as personnel people often come from the S quadrant and personnel people are often involved in the interview process. They will make you feel quite comfortable. Supporters will ask you how your journey was, did you find the place okay, no problem parking etc. They will more often than not offer you a cup of coffee (biscuits too, from the High-S). Their style is to care for the relationship, however brief, so they will outline the game plan, check for understanding and then begin in a friendly non-confrontational way. Because Supporters are generally friendly, non-challenging and easy to talk with, the interviewee may be somewhat misled. *'Oh we got on very well indeed, couldn't have been more helpful and friendly. I think I'm in with a very good chance.'* The Supporter is not being in the least misleading, that is the way they behave with everybody.

A Sales Manager in financial services who had a sound grasp of Personality Profiling once told of a sales force he inherited from his predecessor. He said the atmosphere was very cosy, everyone got on well with everybody else, people asked about each other and expressed concern if anyone was off sick - the only problem amongst these nice people was that nobody was hitting target. The sales manager discovered that the interview process began with the Personnel Department. The Personnel people were virtually all from the Supporter quadrant and they tended to prefer applicants from their own quadrant (we are all capable of it). They found the Ds too forceful, abrupt and lacking in friendly intimacy. The Is they found too noisy and flamboyant and though they had more in common with the Cs a predominance of Ss were chosen. So when the sales manager received the vetted candidates for the second interview, though their experience, qualifications and background varied they were mostly from the same quadrant..

This is not to say that Ss cannot sell. But a sales force needs Drivers in there, people who can assert, 'no time for a chat, I've got some deals to close' or some Is who have the ability and communication skills to do the job (they just need direction). Also the Cs may be low key but their skill is to beaver away at a project. The

C will enter the sales office and quietly mark up a deal on the board whereas the I will ring the company bell, sound the sales horn or photocopy the order and place a copy on everyone's desk. Sure the Supporters can cut the mustard but in an all-S environment that necessary go-in-for-the-kill determination may be non-existent.

Ideally, the sales manager should see the applicants first and let personnel tidy up the details later

The Co-ordinator as Interviewer

It depends very much on which quadrant the interviewee comes from but the C may come across as distant, cool, detached and analytical - a classic C. This could give the applicant the impression that he or she was not doing well. You'll spot the signs early. Cs are not effusive, ebullient or backslapping types. The handshake (if you get one) will not be a bone cruncher. The smile (if you get one) and welcome will be low key. The questions will be specific, detailed and to the point. Generalisations will not go down well. 'Yeah, I spent some time in New York' will only elicit questions about how much time, what were you doing, who did you work for, why did you leave, what were the dates. 'I left because of the pressure' - what pressure, what were your duties, why couldn't you cope, how long, how often, did you give proper notice, did you work that notice (High-Cs like the rule book being followed).

Co-ordinators like facts, accuracy, details, correct chronological sequences and clarity. The interviewee's content will not vary much from quadrant to quadrant but the style and delivery can be adapted to the Interviewer's .

Mr Nice Guy and Mr Nasty

The police may use this tactic when interviewing a suspect. Mr Nice Guy (in a Supporter persona) may soften up the suspect with offers of coffee, cigarettes, enquiries about the family and a level of concern for the suspect's welfare. When Mr S has acquired as much information as he can to get on with, enter Mr Nasty (in a Driver persona) and completely alters the style, maybe offering threats and engendering as much fear as possible. This disorients the suspect and the different line of questioning may evoke a new line of revelation. Re-enter Mr Nice Guy and the suspect may even confide in him that Mr Nasty is a swine. Mr Nice Guy may agree, admitting the man has a fierce record for harshness, which may elicit more pieces of information by virtue of an element of collusion between the two.

This can be disorienting in a job interview. Though not the intentional game plan, interviewees may find one interviewer (personnel perhaps) very agreeable and friendly while that 'other person was a right bastard, horrible manner'.

A good grasp of personality types won't change the world but it will help enormously our perception of it. Understanding is half-way to forgiving. It is when we just cannot understand someone's attitude that our hostility is strongest.

7

Questions and Answers

Which Psychometric Test/Personality Profile would you recommend?

If you pointed at a tool box and asked which implement was the best, the answer has to be 'For What?' You want to drive a nail home? - a hammer. Level a piece of wood? - a plane ... and so forth. There are questionnaires which take as little as 10 minutes to complete (Thomas). Some take around 10-15 minutes (Rapid Personality Questionnaire). The California Psychological Inventory, 309 question version, takes roughly 30 minutes and the 434 question version about 50 minutes. The Sixteen Personality Factor Questionnaire (16PF) will take approx 40 minutes while the Occupational Personality Questionnaire (OPQ), depending on the version, can take anything between 10 and 60 minutes.

The PPA (Personal Profile Analysis) preferred by Thomas International measures 4QB (Four Quadrant Behaviour) in the DISC format which this book devotes the bulk of its content to. Other tests such as the self-explanatory 16PF measures 16 personality factors including *warmth, reasoning, emotional stability, social boldness, vigilance, abstractedness, apprehension and tension.* The longest version of the OPQ measures 30 personality factors including, *affiliative, socially confident, modest, forward planning, worrying, practical, data rational, artistic, behavioural, conceptual, emotional control, active and achieving.*

Some tests are normative and some ipsative. Ipsative questions are answered by a simple Yes or No, alternatively by True or False. Normative tests give a scale, usually 1 to 5 - as in:

I enjoy meeting with lots of new people	**1**	**2**	**3**	**4**	**5**
I am always punctual for appointments	**1**	**2**	**3**	**4**	**5**

Personally, I dislike the five options as it is too easy for the appraisee to opt for the middle figure. An even number demands that we have to opt for one side or the other of the divide.

It has been argued that if you take say, 50 personality factors, you could lay out four paper trays marked **D I S** and **C**, and most if not all of the personality factors could be placed in one of the four trays, thereby negating the need for such a broad spectrum. But this directs us back to the 'For What?' question above. If a company is selecting a candidate for a key position in a high tech, high change industry, then it is wise to cover such factors as *change oriented, conceptual, innovative, emotional control* and other relevant factors as specific issues. A sweeping, *he'll be okay he's a D/I with plenty of drive and an open mind*, may not be good enough. The D/I could by nurture be rather old-fashioned and conventional and if we are looking for a thrusting innovator who thrives on new ideas and revolutionary concepts, the 4QB might not be broad enough.

Finally there is the language. Myers-Briggs Type Indicator (MBTI) sticks with the original Jungian terminology covered earlier. Margerison-McCann's Team Management Systems have a range of descriptive terms for type such as *Explorer Promoter, Assessor Developer, Thruster Organiser, Concluder Producer* and more. Wilson Learning Corporation use 4QB as in *Driver, Expressive, Amiable, Analytical* but these can be subdivided into 16 sub-types such as *Driver/Driver, Expressive/Driver, Amiable/Driver and Analytical/ Driver*, i.e. four types of Driver, four types of Expressive and so on.

Some are veterans in the field such as 16PF introduced in 1949 and both PPA and CPI in the 1950s (though PPA was introduced in the UK in 1980). OPQ was first published in 1984. All of them have a valuable function, like the implements in the tool box, but it depends on what you wish to achieve.

I'm putting together a sales force, what quadrant would you recommend ?

Again more questions. What are you selling? How big is the team? Direct sales or retail sales? Telesales or face-to-face? Selling into private housing or business sales? For example, if domestic sales like the Avon lady or Tupperware, a High-S or High-I could do the job very well indeed. Financial services where the salespeople hammer away at the telephone determined to make an appointment might be more effective with High-Ds and High-Cs. Information Technology sales could benefit from a High-C who would have the natural aptitude for complex detail. If a product is very conceptual, needing picture painting and lots of associated benefits, the Inspirer could be the person for the job.

Take the sale of a mobile home or caravan. All the talk in the world about engine capacity, axle width, acceleration, fibreglass bodywork, BS and ISO standards will be unlikely to clinch the deal. Lots of visual imagery about tranquil highland glens, clear streams, waking up to the sound of birds, peace and communing with nature will help close the deal. Don't mention being channelled into a caravan park with two hundred others parked so close together you can smell each others sausages. Similarly, someone hosting an Anne Summers Underwear and Sex Aid party should not dwell on fabrics, washability, durability, type of elastic or how many batteries a sex toy needs. Battery longevity and cell composition is for police and boy-scout torches. Selling conceptual dreams is not a time for technological specifications. This is High-I (or S territory)

As a generic guide, most selling involves very high rates of rejection, 99 to 1 being common. High-Is tend to have a please-love-me disposition and the constant series of rejections can sometimes be too much for them to take. High-Ds are not so sensitive. When the prospect uses the body-swerve statement 'I need to think about it', the High-D sees this as a buying signal. He'll reply 'Good, so you are obviously interested in the product for you to give it your serious consideration, right?' 'Er, well, yes' 'Good. Now what particular aspect do you need to consider? Is it the technical specification - Is it the payments plan - ('process of elimination' close) - Is it delivery times ...'. 'No I just want to think about it' The High-D persists 'Well that is precisely what I get paid for - to help my clients with any areas of grey they may have - now, what is it that I haven't covered fully enough?'

It takes a relatively hard closer to keep working away. It also takes an intelligent balance of appearing not quite to understand what the prospect needs to know and being so persistent as to alienate the prospect. The High-C could also pursue this line of closing, appearing slightly askance in perhaps having failed to be totally clear in the sales presentation.

The High-S and High-I dislike confrontation, they want to be friends. The sympathetic Supporter when confronted with 'I want to think about it' has an inclination to respond with 'naturally, of course you do'. Only experience and discipline will curb this personality preference.

Another generic point is that if you are recruiting a large direct sales team it is probably better to have a **balanced** team because they all can learn from each other's styles and on occasion swap a sales call because of a better personality match.

I need to be more assertive - would an assertiveness course help?

Very probably. It is important that such a course does not set out to change your natural style. The dominant father tries this with a passive son. *Pull yourself together; Be a man; Stand up for yourself; Don't be such a wimp.* Hopeless, all the father will do is create a bigger rift. Like Prince Edward's despatch into the Royal Marines (familiarly known in the RN as *Bootnecks*). To use the old cliché, you cannot put a square peg in a round hole.

The best approach to becoming more assertive is first to recognise your own quadrant. Check all your own strengths and weaknesses and acknowledge them. Once you have the core 'you', it is then possible to build upon it. The High-D in a restaurant when served with tepid soup will be heard wall to wall, *'Hey! This soup is cold!'*. The Supporter would shy away from such an in-your-face challenge. But what is the objective of assertiveness? To get what you want. So whether you adopt a persona or use your own natural style in an assertive way matters not, so long as you get hot soup.

Before we continue, a word here on nurture. Americans have a simple philosophy - I pay you good money - you give me good service. Easy. If the soup is cold, it is no big deal, the American will draw attention to it - this is wrong, get it right. The customer expects it, the waiter expects it, the chef expects it, the Maitre D' expects it, nobody takes offence. It gets put right. The Brits however are a complex lot. It has much to do with nurture, i.e. the hierarchical class structure of British (mainly English) society; knowing 'one's place' - 'I don't like to make a fuss or order people about.' (That's the right of the rich and posh - 'not for the likes of us').

Although the wounds of class division have healed, the scars remain. Paradoxically, the more expensive the restaurant, the more passive Brits can become whereas one would expect the opposite. If you are spending serious money, you should demand seriously good service. But Brits can become intimidated by an immaculate Maitre D' and sumptuous surroundings (why? for God's sake - you are paying for it) and they can even end up whispering to each other if some ultra-posh accents are wittering on at full volume (their natural entitlement of course, denied to the plebs).

When complaining, the English may actually begin by apologising. *'Excuse me, sorry to bother you, I don't like to make a fuss, but I wonder would it be at all possible to have this steak done a little longer, it is just a little too rare for me'*. The waiter examines the piece of raw meat swimming in a pool of blood and (knowing the English passiveness) asks, *'Didn't you ask for it rare?'* The subtext is clear - this is what you asked for, why can't you make your mind up, you are a nuisance. Reluctantly he takes it away, *'Right, madam, I'll tell the chef'*. Who cares what she ordered, if the woman is not happy, make her happy. Do not question paying customers.

So if you are the diametric opposite of an Assertive, i.e. a Supporter, and service is not good enough, first never be apologetic. *'You repaired these shoes on Wednesday and the heel fell off this one the following day'*. No need to say anything else, the onus is on the repairman to respond. *'Waiter, this soup is only just tepid'*. A calm factual statement is better than a hostile one. Why have a bad relationship with the staff when it could spoil your precious and expensive evening. Anger is not only counterproductive but is invariably misplaced. The waiter didn't prepare tepid soup, the chef did. The shop assistant didn't make your electrical appliance faulty, the manufacturer did.

A popular way of evoking the best response from a complaint is the High-Low-High approach, that is, go in with a positive - deliver the negative - finish on a positive. This can be used most effectively in management when having to tell off an employee. *'George, your work is generally very thorough and professional but this report is really very scrappy and carelessly put together'*. Wait for the response which will take in the fault and the compliment together, i.e. *'Yes it wasn't my best effort but the deadline was very tight'*. Then you can finish on a high, *'Not enough time, eh? Okay but let me know in future, don't submit shoddy work, you are far too good for that.'* Point made; egos salvaged; no offence given or taken. It can also be used humorously as in the shoe repair. *'You repaired these shoes yesterday. The soles are brilliant; I'm happy with the soles - but the heels fell off.'* You'll get the result you want and maybe even a smile from the repairman.

The trouble with many situations where one has to be assertive is nerves. People get uptight. The more tense you are the more it is transmitted to the recipient. This can make the atmosphere fraught and the outcome more hostile than necessary. So the high-low-high (or just high-low) can make it easier. *'Waiter, the flavour of this soup is excellent, however it is a bit too cold'*. There is no need to dot the 'i's or cross the 't's, exaggerate or be repetitive. *'I bought this toaster yesterday and it doesn't work'*. No need for 'and another thing' or 'not only that but ...' Neither over-assert nor under-assert, just state the facts. In the Navy, the rule when having to verbally discipline a sailor was, *Say it once, say it clear and shut your face*. What it lacks in finesse it makes up for in clarity and logic.

Jung says that 4QB Types are universal. How come men are more violent than women?

There is a correlation between aggression and the Dominant quadrant, however violence enters another realm. Researchers led by Prof. Dan Ely at the University of Akron in Ohio found that the Y chromosome, otherwise referred to as the male chromosome, contains genes which, when stimulated, reduce the levels of serotonin, an important chemical neurotransmitter that carries messages between neurones in the brain and influences mood. They found levels of the male hormone testosterone increased which resulted in a higher level of aggression.

So although there is a personality factor, the males' tendency to fight is more a matter of biochemistry or their genetic make-up rather than their DISC quadrant.

Are there other gender differences ?

Plenty. When Allan Pease (the body language expert) and Barbara Pease were working on their book *Why Men Don't Listen and Women Can't Read Maps*, they observed, 'Society today is determined to believe that men and women possess exactly the same skills, aptitudes and potential - just as science is beginning to prove they are completely different'. Airlines refused to tell the Peases why fewer than 1% of pilots are female. A motoring organisation proved conclusively that men are better at reverse-parking than women. The report was suppressed. The academics who spoke to the Peases would only do so 'off the record' and anonymously, lest they appeared politically incorrect. The fear is of an inferior/superior implication while the answer is much simpler, we just happen to be different.

Women have far better sensory skills, higher levels of brain activity and wider peripheral vision (more boys than girls are knocked down by cars). Women are better at 'multi-track' thinking and can remember all those convoluted family connections, children's names, lists and so forth. They make better secretaries, receptionists and customer complaint handlers - not sexism, just sheer competence.

Men are stronger at linear problem-solving and spatial or numerical skills, hence their predominance as architects, accountants, pilots or composers. Pure logic would dictate that if we all thought the same way and were driven by the same motivating forces, the numbers of children born then cared for till their teens would decline even more sharply than is currently the case. On the down side, the Peases reveal a survey which shows that the more women are urged to compete with men, whether in the boardroom, the battlefield or in the professions, the higher the incidence of mainly male fringe benefits such as heart disease, lung cancer, ulcers, stress and premature death.

My company's culture is very High-D. The macho, hairy-chested style of management is very much the norm but it's not my style. Adapt or go?

This is an increasingly common problem. Globalisation means companies can relocate to chase higher productivity and lower operating costs. Old fashioned concepts such as loyalty, consideration and honour are being sacrificed on the altar of profit. CEOs can be awarded bonuses and share options worth millions. For what? For engendering a brilliant working atmosphere, for high standards of customer care, for the highest standards of business ethic? Sadly no.

Recently the CEO of Britain's Barclay's Bank announced a 30 per cent surge in profits. The shareholders were delighted with their windfall. How was it achieved? By axing 7,500 jobs; and the CEO wants to achieve more cuts in the region of £1 billion. How? Cutting more jobs by shutting hundreds of High Street branches. This is a random example but could have been any major corporation. The shareholders demand results, the Chairman and Board of Directors send out directives; regional managers get their orders and pass them to on to line managers. The whole dynamic becomes numbers driven. Sales managers set targets for sales teams. Individuals carry their own targets. The individual reports his results to his team leader - team leader to manager - manager to regional manager and finally back to the men with the big charts in the Board Room. Despite the wisdom of John Adair's TTI dynamic, commercial forces are making us more stressed rather than less. The need to 'perform' is paramount and the tendency to appoint managers of a Dominant disposition is growing.

If you are a line manager and the company style is to gather your teams together and hector them, threaten them and even ridicule them, you have a problem if this style is anathema to you. We've all witnessed it in some form, the (probably) Supporter line manager has been roared at by the Driver boss and told to read The Riot Act to the troops 'in no uncertain manner'. You can adapt to this style on occasion but you can't expect to adopt it permanently. Any prolonged splitting of your personality will result in stress. The Driver prefers the bombastic style, he doesn't really want dialogue. The Supporter needs dialogue and interaction. One method in the Supporter style might be,

'Chris, you had a lousy month, come up here and tell us all what you did and didn't do and how you reckon you will hit target next month'

This way you can make a meeting more consultative. Involve others. *'Anyone want to suggest what Chris might do to handle this problem?'*

The Dominant would find this consultative approach soft and wimpish. You can hear him - *'This isn't a damn AA meeting or the marriage guidance council. Tell them the results you want and if they can't shape up, ship out.'*

It may take a degree of courage and determination to say 'No, I'll do it my way', but it beats the alternative of putting on your chest wig at every meeting and acting the tough guy. Moreover, apart from the stress, it doesn't work. The troops spot someone acting out of character immediately and any element of strength and conviction is lost. So save yourself the apprehension, the butterflies in the stomach (which will turn to acid pain in time) and the risk of looking foolish and losing respect. A real S has to be superior to a plastic D.

My kids are both Feelers. They are into everything. Can I make them more like Thinkers?

No.

But they really are unstoppable. They wear me out.

If it is just pronounced exploratory behaviour consistent with, say, a

Sensing Feeler that's the way it is. But if behaviour is too far over the top, then a child could be hyperactive and medical opinion would be necessary to determine if so.

Which tools would you recommend in the recruitment process?
One pitfall employers are learning to be wary of is The Data Protection Act 1998. In force since March 2000, but certain types of data were exempt until October 2001. These exemptions no longer apply. Under the Act, any job applicant may now be able to access interview notes, also any seemingly innocuous hand written comments which have made their way into a personnel filing system. Score sheets from psychometric tests may also be accessed and the results of any other tests, numeric, literacy, comprehension and so on. Documentation may then be scrutinised for evidence of any unreasonable bias, especially gender, racial, ethnic or ageist. Failure to comply could result in an action for contempt of court.

Further, all such documentation must be retained for a period of not less than four months after the recruitment decision has been made. Most recruiters remain unaware of this and they are also unaware that in application documents, the candidates should be advised of their rights. Applicants to job vacancies are entitled to know to whom their CV or application form is being directed. For example, at the time of writing, in 2002, the Scottish Arts Council required job applicants to submit not one but four copies of CVs and four copies of the completed application form with no indication as to whom they would be distributed. Apart from being a breach of the Act, in the village-like atmosphere of Edinburgh where everyone knows everyone else in that tiny square half-mile of the business district, it is bad policy in so far as it makes applicants in existing jobs apprehensive lest they become the focus of discussion. When recruiting, the advice of Murray McCall, an employment law specialist and senior associate at McRoberts Solicitors is, 'as a rule of thumb, recruiters would be advised not to write anything about anyone which they cannot justify objectively or would not want them to see.'

So much for the law and what not to do. To most mature,

perceptive and humanitarian recruiters, the best tool of all is to ask for a letter from applicants in which they should outline their understanding of the job and why they believe they have the necessary skills, experience and attitude to handle the work. Ask them to outline their career to date, their interests, achievements, disappointments or any facet of their character and experience which they feel relevant. This provides a broad and blank canvass. It is up to the applicant to make a presentation. A letter can convey style, humour, education, literacy, humanity, warmth (or lack of it), strength, motivation, enthusiasm and a whole host of qualities which die on the page of an application form. As stressed earlier in the book, application forms with endless wee boxes which ask about primary education, 'O' Levels, referees and details from leaving school onwards may be of some interest but you can capture the character and first impression of an individual in a letter.

The referee tool nowadays is almost valueless. People change jobs much more frequently. The personnel staff in the company which you left several years ago have probably all moved on. The line manager you reported to is with a new company and the only contact who remembers you is reluctant to make any categoric comment in writing. Make your own judgements. If you feel the burning need to acquire third party referrals, your gut feeling is probably telling you that something is not quite right.

Sure, ask for a CV to accompany the letter but application forms are for large, lazy organisations who want the world to conform to their template.

Psychometric Tests are a good tool but they should be *job specific*. Whether a toll collector on the Forth Bridge is a D, I, S or C is of no relevance. A numeracy test might be useful though. Giving change for £10 when taking a fiver (or vice versa) might not auger well for long service in the tollbooth. Not only is it desirable that such tests be job specific but under the Data Protection Act they must be job specific.

I sit on several committees and often have trouble keeping harmony. Any advice?

More committees experience disharmony and friction because of clashes of personality than they do over substantive issues under discussion. Committees are peculiar things. Some people are attracted to them simply because they are committees and it may appeal to a certain level of self-importance (Maslow's Level 3). Other people may have time on their hands and perhaps a rather solitary life and are motivated to join for a level of companionship or stimulation (Maslow's Level 2). Some talk too much and others say very little. From the Four Quadrant Behaviour aspect, committees are ideal observation forums to watch personality in action.

The **Dominant** will want to get started. *Right now, if everybody's here, let's crack on and get started.* You can just hear him - and it's usually a him, often from the Captain Mainwaring school of management.

The **Inspirer** is still shaking hands with the others, chatting and being amiably communicative.

The **Supporter** wants to know if everyone has a cup of tea or other refreshment along with expressing other areas of concern, *How's your chest Mr Brocklebank? You had a very nasty cough at the last meeting.*

The **Coordinator** will check everyone has a copy of the minutes. There is no need to check for spelling mistakes as the C probably not only took the minutes but typed them as well.

When the meeting starts the D and the I will want to press on with the agenda. However the C will interrupt to ask, *Any apologies?* then insist that the previous minutes have been read and understood. The I will nod and say 'Yeah, yeah', without any attempt to ensure the minutes were an accurate record of the proceedings. The C, having burnt the midnight oil typing the minutes will ask, with a degree of exasperation, if the I wishes to vote that the minutes be accepted. The I puts his hand up unhesitatingly. The C then asks for someone to second the vote. The S likes to be cautious and doesn't wish to upset anyone, so holds fire. Any other Cs are carefully re-reading the minutes to check their veracity. Predictably the D puts his hand up.

Right, let us move on to item one on the agenda, says the Chair. Just a moment, says the C, should we not see if there are any 'matters arising'?

The pattern is precisely the same in just about any committee meeting. The Inspirers will tend to make loose generalisations and be faulted by the Coordinators for a lack of precision. The C may consider the I a sloppy and undisciplined thinker and the I is irritated by what he sees as the Cs constant nit-picking pedantry. If they clash over such detail, the D will start to drum his fingers impatiently while the S will want to restore harmony and will endeavour to be a peace-maker.

There is no easy way out of this situation. In the business world, there are a few disciplines which might be useful

1. The meeting must have an objective. No point just having a fixed interval meeting just for the sake of it.
2. Minutes and current agenda must be distributed in advance. All too often the first glimpse people have of the agenda is when they take their seat at the meeting. When people know what is to be discussed they can prepare; the same with any comment on the minutes of the preceding meeting.
3. There should be no need for Any Other Business. If the agenda is distributed in time, then people can suggest inclusions in advance.

Do we need such detailed personality identities ?

Most of the time, no. We all get by saying, *He's a bit of a clam. She's very outgoing and exuberant. He's very abrupt and impatient. She is so caring:* and the endless number of permutations of the same. However there are times when accurate specifics are essential. In the Introduction, one quote was, try walking into your local garage and asking for some blue touch-up paint. Those unfamiliar with the motor industry's paint shades may be surprised to learn that from pale blue or sky blue to navy blue or midnight blue there are roughly twenty intermediate shades each with their own imaginative type names. As the lyric from the Irish song has it, There's forty shades of green. Similarly, the average commuter on the No 31 bus will settle for being told, 'It's going to be windy'. Such a description would be of no use to a sailor putting to sea. Gales, storms and hurricanes are all denoted by specific force numbers on the Beaufort Scale just as earth tremors are registered on the Richter Scale. Precision of use can be literally a matter of life or death.

With personality, a Sales Manager might interview someone who is loosely an Inspirer but a more precise profile could be decisive. Is the applicant an Inspiring Driver or and Inspiring Supporter? In a 50/50 situation, most managers would prefer the former. A caring Supporter might make a good medical receptionist, however a Supporting Coordinator might be a better choice than a Supporting Inspirer.

Surely a good actor could convey any personality type ?

To a degree. Rock Hudson was the epitome of big butch American manhood yet privately he had quite an extravagantly gay lifestyle. Most of his fans were shocked to learn of his sexuality. Brando conveyed real menace in *The Wild Ones*, macho explosiveness in *A Streetcar Named Desire*; decency, honour with a touch of foppishness in *Mutiny on the Bounty*, but such consummate versatility is rare. All movie directors, casting directors, stage managers and the general public know the dangers of miscasting.

Most of the great performances occur when the actor's personality is close to the character's. Dirk Bogarde's greatest triumphs were playing sensitive, brooding, thoughtful roles with perhaps his best work being in *Death In Venice*. His one or two attempts at tough guys lacked conviction. John Wayne, one of cinema's biggest stars, became so typecast playing John Wayne that it would have been impossible for him to play any role requiring great delicacy or sensitivity.

Perhaps the last word should go to Carl Gustav Jung. His central theme was that mental illness was characterised by disunity of the personality, while mental health is manifested by unity *towards which the personality strives.*

Index